The Business of Being a Woman

by Ida M. Tarbell

INTRODUCTION

The object of this little volume is to call attention to a certain distrust, which the author feels in the modern woman, of the significance and dignity of the work laid upon her by Nature and by society. Its ideas are the result of a long, if somewhat desultory, observation of the professional, political, and domestic activities of women in this country and in France. These observations have led to certain definite opinions as to those phases of the woman question most in need of emphasis to-day.

A great problem of human life is to preserve faith in and zest for everyday activities. The universal easily becomes the vulgar and the burdensome. The highest civilization is that in which the largest number sense, and are so placed as to realize, the dignity and the beauty of the common experiences and obligations.

* * * * *

The courtesy of the publishers of the American Magazine, in permitting the use here of chapters which have appeared in that periodical, is gratefully acknowledged.

TABLE OF CONTENTS

CHAPTER

THE BUSINESS OF BEING A WOMAN

CHAPTER I

The Uneasy Woman

The most conspicuous occupation of the American woman of to-day, dressing herself aside, is self-discussion. It is a disquieting phenomenon. Chronic self-discussion argues chronic ferment of mind, and ferment of mind is a serious handicap to both happiness and efficiency. Nor is self-discussion the only exhibit of restlessness the American woman gives. To an unaccustomed observer she seems always to be running about on the face of things with no other purpose than to put in her time. He points to the triviality of the things in which she can immerse herself--her fantastic and ever-changing raiment, the welter of lectures and other culture schemes which she supports, the eagerness with which she transports herself to the ends of the earth--as marks of a spirit not at home with itself, and certainly not convinced that it is going in any particular direction or that it is committed to any particular worth-while task.

Perhaps the most disturbing side of the phenomenon is that it is coincident with the emancipation of woman. At a time when she is freer than at any other period of the world's history--save perhaps at one period in ancient Egypt--she is apparently more uneasy.

Those who do not like the exhibit are inclined to treat her as if she were a new historical type. The reassuring fact is, that ferment of mind is no newer thing in woman than in man. It is a human ailment. Its attacks, however, have always been unwelcome. Society distrusts uneasiness in sacred quarters; that is, in her established and privileged works. They are the best mankind has to show for itself. At least they are the things for which the race has slaved longest and which so far have best resisted attack. We would like to pride ourselves that they were permanent, that we had settled some things. And hence society resents a restless woman. And this is logical enough.

Embroiled as man is in an eternal effort to conquer, understand, and reduce to order both nature and his fellows, it is imperative that he have some secure spot where his head is not in danger, his heart is not harassed.

Woman, by virtue of the business nature assigns her, has always been theoretically the maker and keeper of this necessary place of peace. But she has rarely made it and kept it with full content. Eve was a revolt 閑, so was Medea. In every century they have appeared, restless Amazons, protesting and remolding. Out of their uneasy souls have come the varying changes in the woman's world which distinguish the ages.

Society has not liked it--was there to be no quiet anywhere? It is poor understanding that does not appreciate John Adams' parry of his wife Abigail's list of grievances, which she declared the Continental Congress must relieve if it would avoid a woman's rebellion. Under the stress of the Revolution children, apprentices, schools, colleges, Indians, and negroes had all become insolent and turbulent, he told her. What was to become of the country if women, "the most numerous and powerful tribe in the world," grew discontented?

Now this world-old restlessness of the women has a sound and a tragic cause. Nature lays a compelling hand on her. Unless she obeys freely and fully she must pay in unrest and vagaries. For the normal woman the fulfillment of life is the making of the thing we best describe as a home--which means a mate, children, friends, with all the radiating obligations, joys, burdens, these relations imply.

This is nature's plan for her; but the home has got to be founded inside the imperfect thing we call society. And these two, nature and society, are continually getting into each other's way, wrecking each other's plans, frustrating each other's schemes. The woman almost never is able to adjust her life so as fully to satisfy both. She is between two fires. Euripides understood this when he put into Medea's mouth a cry as modern as any that Ibsen has conceived:--

Of all things upon earth that grow, A herb most bruised is woman. We must pay Our store of gold, hoarded for that one day, To buy us some man's love; and lo, they bring A master of our flesh! There comes the sting Of the whole shame. And then the jeopardy, For good or ill, what shall that master be; 'Tis magic she must have or prophecy-- Home never taught her that--how best to guide Toward peace this thing that sleepeth at her side. And she who, laboring long, shall find some way Whereby her lord may bear with her, nor fray His yoke too fiercely, blessed is the breath That woman draws!

Medea's difficulty was that which is oftenest in the way of a woman carrying her business in life to a satisfactory completion--false mating. It is not a difficulty peculiar to woman. Man knows it as often. It is the heaviest curse society brings on human beings--the most fertile cause of apathy, agony, and failure. If the woman's cry is more poignant under it than the man's, it is because the machine which holds them both allows him a wider sweep, more interests outside of their immediate alliance. "A man, when he is vexed at home," complains Medea, "can go out and find relief among his friends or acquaintances, but we women have none to look at but him."

And when it is impossible longer to "look" at him, what shall she do! Tell her woe to the world, seek a soporific, repudiate the scheme of things, or from the vantage point of her failure turn to the untried relations of her life, call upon her unused powers?

From the beginning of time she has tried each and all of these methods of meeting her purely human woe. At times the women of whole peoples have sunk into apathy, their business reduced to its dullest, grossest forms. Again, whole groups have taken themselves out of the partnership which both Nature and Society have ordered. The Amazons refused to recognize man as an equal and mated simply that they might rear more women like themselves. Here the tables were turned and the boy baby turned out--not to the wolves, but to man! The convent has always been a favorite way of escape.

It has never been a majority of women who for a great length of time have shirked this problem by any one of these methods. By individuals and by groups woman has always been seeking to develop the business of life to such proportions, to so diversify, refine, and broaden it that no half failure or utter failure of its fundamental relations would swamp her, leave her comfortless, or prevent her working out that family which she knew to be her part in the scheme of things. It is from her conscious attempt to make the best of things when they are proved bad, that there has come the uneasiness which trails along her path from Eve to Mrs. Pankhurst.

When great changes have come in the social system, her quest has responded to them, taken its color and direction from them. The peculiar forms of uneasiness in the American woman of to-day come naturally enough from the Revolution of 1776. That movement upset theoretically everything which had been expected of her before. Theoretically, it broke down the division fences which had kept her in sets and groups. She was no longer to be a woman of class; she was a woman of the people. This was striking at the very underpinning of femininity, as the world knew it. Theoretically, too, her ears were no longer to be closed to all ideas save those of her church or party,--a new thing, freedom of speech, was abroad,--her lips were opened with man's. Moreover, her business of family building was modified, as well as her attitude towards life. The necessity of all women educating themselves that they might be able to educate their children was an obligation on the face of the new undertaking. Another revolutionary duty put upon her was--paying her way. There can be no real democracy where there is parasitism. She must achieve conscious independence whether in or out of the family. Unquestionably there came with the Revolution a vision of a new woman--a woman from whom all of the willfulness and frivolity and helplessness of the "Lady" of the old r 間 ime should be stripped, while all her qualities of gentleness and charm should be preserved. The old-world lady was to be merged into a woman strong, capable, severely beautiful, a creature who had all of the virtues and none of the follies of femininity.

It was strong yeast they put into the pot in '76.

A fresh leaven in a people can never be distributed evenly. Moreover, the mass to which it is applied is never homogeneous. There are spots so hard no yeast can move them; there are others so light the yeast burns them out. Taken as a whole, the change is labored and painful. So our new notions worked on women. There were groups which resented and refused them, became reactionary at the stating of them. There were those which grew grave and troubled under them, shrinking from the portentous upheaval they felt in their touch, yet sensing that they must be accepted. There were still others where the notion frothed and foamed, turning up unexpected ideas, revealing depths of dissatisfaction, of desire, of unsuspected powers in woman that startled the staid old world. It was in these quarters that there was produced the uneasy woman typical of the day.

Her ferment went to the bottom of things this time. Not since the age of the Amazon had a body of women broken more utterly with things as they are.

And like the Amazon, the revolt was against man and his pretensions.

It was no unorganized revolt. It was deliberate. It presented her case in a carefully prepared List of Grievances, and an eloquent Declaration of Sentiments[1] both adopted in a strictly parliamentary way, and made the basis of an organized revolt, which has gone on systematically ever since. The essence of her complaint, as embodied in the above expression, is that man is a conscious tyrant holding woman an unwilling captive--cutting her off from the things in life which really matter: education, freedom of speech, the ballot; that she can never be his equal until she does the same things her tyrant does, studies the book he studies, practices the trades and professions he practices, works with him in government.

The inference from all this is that the Business of Being a Woman, as it has been conducted heretofore by society, is of less importance than the Business of Being a Man, and that the time has come to enter his world and prove her equality.

There are certain assumptions in her program which will bear examination. Is man the calculating tyrant the modern uneasy woman charges? Are her fetters due only to his unfair domination? Or is she suffering from the generally bungling way things go in the world? And is not man a victim as well as she--caught in the same trap? Moreover, is woman never a tyrant? One of the first answers to her original revolt came from the most eminent woman of the day, Harriet Beecher Stowe, and it was called "Pink and White Tyranny!" "I have seen a collection of medieval English poems," says Chesterton, "in which the section headed 'Poems of Domestic Life' consisted entirely (literally entirely) of the complaints of husbands bullied by their wives."

Again, will doing the same things a man does work as well in stifling her unrest as she fancies it has in man's case? If a woman's temperamental and intellectual operations were identical with a man's, there would be hope of success,--but they are not. She is a different being. Whether she is better or worse, stronger or weaker, primary or secondary, is not the question. She is different.

And she tries to ease a world-old human curse by imitating the occupations, points of views, and methods of a radically different being. Can she realize her quest in this way? Generally speaking, nothing is more wasteful in human operations than following a course which is not native and spontaneous, not according to the law of the being.

If she demonstrates her points, successfully copies man's activities, can she impress her program on any great body of women? The mass of women believe in their task. Its importance is not capable of argument in their minds. Nor do they see themselves dwarfed by their business. They know instinctively that under no other circumstances can such ripeness and such wisdom be developed, that nowhere else is the full nature called upon, nowhere else are there such intricate, delicate, and intimate forces in play, calling and testing them.

To bear and to rear, to feel the dependence of man and child--the necessity for themselves--to know that upon them depend the health, the character, the happiness, the future of certain human beings--to see themselves laying and preserving the foundations of so imposing a thing as a family--to build so that this family shall become a strong stone in the state--to feel themselves through this family perpetuating and perfecting church, society, republic,-- this is their destiny,--this is worth while. They may not be able to state it, but all their instincts and experiences convince them of the supreme and eternal value of their place in the world. They dare not tamper with it. Their opposition to the militant program badly and even cruelly expressed at times has at bottom, as an opposition always has, the principle of preservation. It is not bigotry or vanity or a petty notion of their own spheres which has kept the majority of women from lending themselves to the radical wing of the woman's movement. It is fear to destroy a greater thing which they possess. The fear of change is not an irrational thing--the fear of change is founded on the risk of losing what you have, on the certainty of losing much temporarily at least. It sees the cost, the ugly and long period of transition.

Moreover, respect for your calling brings patience with its burden and its limitations. The change you desire you work for conservatively, if at all. The women who opposed the first movement for women's rights in this country might deplore the laws that gave a man the power to beat his wife--but as a matter of fact few men did beat their wives, and popular opinion was a powerful weapon. They might deplore the laws of property--but few of them were deeply touched by them. The husband, the child, the home, the social circle, the church, these things were infinitely more interesting and important to them than diplomas, rights to work, rights to property, rights to vote. All the sentiments in the revolting women's program seemed trivial, cold, profitless beside the realities of life as they dreamed them and struggled to realize them.

It is this same intuitive loyalty to her Business of Being a Woman, her unwillingness to have it tampered with, that is to-day the great obstacle to our Uneasy Woman putting her program of relief into force. And it is the effort to move this mass which she derides as inert that leads to much of the overemphasis in her program and her methods. If she is to attract attention, she must be extreme. The campaigner is like the actor--he must exaggerate to get his effect over the footlights. Moreover, there are natures like that of the actor who could not play Othello unless his whole body was blackened. Nor is the extravagance of the methods, which the militant lady follows to put over her program, so foreign to her nature as it may seem. The suffragette adapts to her needs a form of feminine coquetry as old as the world. To defy and denounce the male has always been one of woman's most successful provocative ways!

However much certain of the assumptions in her program may seem to be against its success, there is much for it. It gives her a scapegoat--an outside, personal, attackable cause for the limitations and defeats she suffers. And there is no greater consolation than fixing blame. It is half a cure in itself to know or to think you know the cause of your difficulties. Moreover, it gives her a scapegoat against whom it is easy to make up a case. She knows him too well, much better than he knows her, much better than she knows herself; at least her knowledge of him is better formulated. And she has this advantage: custom makes it cowardly for a man to attempt to demonstrate that woman is a tyrant--it laughs and applauds woman's attempt to fix the charge on man.

It gives her a definite program of relief. To attack life as man does: to secure the same kind of training, enter a trade or profession where she can support herself, mingle with the crowd as he does, get into politics--that she assumes to be the practical way of curing the inferiority of position and of powers which she is willing to admit, even willing to demonstrate. That a man's life may not be altogether satisfactory, she declines to believe. The uneasy woman has always taken it for granted that man is happier than woman. It is an assumption which is at least discussible.

Her program, too, has the immense advantage of including all that the new order of things in this country, instituted by the Revolution, made imperative for women--the schooling, the liberty of action, the independent pocket book. Because she has formulated these notions so definitely and has hammered on them so hard, the militant woman frequently claims that they originated with her, that she is the cause of the great development in educational opportunities, in freedom to work and to circulate, in the increasing willingness to face the facts of life and speak the truth. This claim she should drop. She is rather the logical result of these notions, their extreme expression. She has, however, had an enormous influence in keeping them alive in the great slow-moving mass of women, where the fate of new ideas rests and where they are always tried out with extreme caution. Without her the vision of enlarging and liberalizing their own particular business to meet the needs of the New Democracy which so exalted the women of the Revolution, would not to-day be as nearly realized as it is. To speak slightingly of her part in the women's movement is uncomprehending. She was then, and always has been, a tragic figure, this woman in the front of the woman's movement--driven by a great unrest, sacrificing old ideals to attain new, losing herself in a frantic and frequently blind struggle, often putting back her cause by the sad illustration she was of the price that must be paid to attain a result. Certainly no woman who to-day takes it as a matter of course that she should study what she chooses, go and come as she will, support herself unquestioned by trade, profession, or art, work in public or private, handle her own property, share her children on equal terms with her husband, receive a respectful attention on platform or before legislature, live freely in the world, should think with anything but reverence particularly of the early disturbers of convention and peace, for they were an essential element in the achievement.

The great strength of the radical program is now, as it has always been, the powerful appeal it makes to the serious young woman. Man and marriage are a trap--that is the essence the young woman draws from the campaign for woman's rights. All the vague terror which at times runs through a girl's dream of marriage, the sudden vision of probable agonies, of possible failure and death, become under the teachings of the militant woman so many realities. She sees herself a "slave," as the jargon has it, putting all her eggs into one basket with the certainty that some, perhaps all, will be broken.

The new gospel offers an escape from all that. She will be a "free" individual, not one "tied" to a man. The "drudgery" of the household she will exchange for what she conceives to be the broad and inspiring work which men are doing. For the narrow life of the family she will escape to the excitement and triumph of a "career." The Business of Being a Woman becomes something to be apologized for. All over the land there are women with children clamoring about them, apologizing for never having done anything! Women whose days are spent in trade and professions complacently congratulate themselves that they at least have lived. There were girls in the early days of the movement, as there no doubt are to-day, who prayed on their knees that they might escape the frightful isolation of marriage, might be free to "live" and to "work," to "know" and to "do."

What it was really all about they never knew until it was too late. That is, they examined neither the accusations nor the premises. They accepted them. Strong young natures are quick to accept charges of injustice. To them it is unnatural that life should be hampered, that it should be anything but radiant. Curing injustice, too, seems particularly easy to the young. It is simply a matter of finding a remedy and putting it into force! The young American woman of militant cast finds it is easy to believe that the Business of Being a Woman is slavery. She has her mother's pains and sacrifices and tears before her, and she resents them. She meets the theory on every hand that the distress she loathes is of man's doing, that it is for her to revolt, to enter his business, and so doing escape his tyranny, find a worth-while life for herself, and at the same time help "liberate" her sex.

And so for sixty years she has been working on this thesis. That she has not demonstrated it sufficiently to satisfy even herself is shown by the fact that she is still the most conspicuous of Uneasy Women. But that she has produced a type and an influential one is certain. Indeed, she may be said to have demonstrated sufficiently for practical purposes what there is for her in imitating the activities of man.

FOOTNOTES:

[1] DECLARATION OF SENTIMENTS

When, in the course of human events, it becomes necessary for one portion of the family of man to assume among the people of the earth a position different from that which they have hitherto occupied, but one to which the laws of nature and of nature's God entitles them, a decent respect to the opinions of mankind requires that they should declare the causes that impel them to such a course.

We hold these truths to be self-evident: that all men and women are created equal; that they are endowed by their Creator with certain inalienable rights; that among these are life, liberty, and the pursuit of happiness; that to secure these rights governments are instituted, deriving their just power from the consent of the governed. Whenever any form of government becomes destructive of these ends, it is the right of those who suffer from it to refuse allegiance to it, and to insist upon the institution of a new government, laying its foundation on such principles, and organizing its powers in such form, as to them shall seem most likely to effect their safety and happiness. Prudence, indeed, will dictate that governments long established should not be changed for light and transient causes; and accordingly all experience hath shown that mankind are more disposed to suffer, while evils are sufferable, than to right themselves by abolishing the forms to which they were accustomed. But when a long train of abuses and usurpations, pursuing invariably the same object, evinces a design to reduce them under absolute despotism, it is their duty to throw off such government, and to provide new guards for their future security. Such has been the patient sufferance of the women under this government, and such is now the necessity which constrains them to demand the equal station to which they are entitled.

The history of mankind is a history of repeated injuries and usurpations on the part of man towards woman, having in direct object the establishment of an absolute tyranny over her. To prove this, let facts be submitted to a candid world.

He has never permitted her to exercise her inalienable right to the elective franchise.

He has compelled her to submit to laws, in the formation of which she has no voice.

He has withheld from her rights which are given to the most ignorant and degraded men--both natives and foreigners.

Having deprived her of this first right of a citizen, the elective franchise, thereby leaving her without representation in the halls of legislation, he has oppressed her on all sides.

He has made her, if married, in the eyes of the law, civilly dead.

He has taken from her all right in property, even to the wages she earns.

He has made her, morally, an irresponsible being, as she can commit many crimes with impunity, provided they be done in the presence of her husband. In the covenant of marriage, she is compelled to promise obedience to her husband, he becoming, to all intents and purposes, her master--the law giving him power to deprive her of her liberty, and to administer chastisement.

He has so framed the laws of divorce, as to what shall be the proper causes, and in case of separation, to whom the guardianship of the children shall be given, as to be wholly regardless of the happiness of women--the law, in all cases, going upon a false supposition of the supremacy of man, and giving all power into his hands.

After depriving her of all rights as a married woman, if single, and the owner of property, he has taxed her to support a government which recognizes her only when her property can be made profitable to it.

He has monopolized nearly all the profitable employments, and from those she is permitted to follow, she receives but a scanty remuneration. He closes against her all the avenues to wealth and distinction which he considers most honorable to himself. As a teacher of theology, medicine, or law, she is not known.

He has denied her the facilities for obtaining a thorough education, all colleges being closed against her.

He allows her in Church, as well as State, but a subordinate position, claiming Apostolic authority for her exclusion from the ministry, and, with some exception, from any public participation in the affairs of the Church.

He has created a false sentiment by giving to the world a different code of morals for men and women, by which moral delinquencies which exclude women from society are not only tolerated, but deemed of little account in man.

He has usurped the prerogative of Jehovah himself, claiming it as his right to assign for her a sphere of action, when that belongs to her conscience and to her God.

He has endeavored, in every way that he could, to destroy her confidence in her own powers, to lessen her self-respect, and to make her willing to lead a dependent and abject life.

CHAPTER II

ON THE IMITATION OF MAN

Fresh attacks on life, like chemical experiments, turn up unexpected by-products. The Uneasy Woman, driven by the thirst for greater freedom, and believing man's way of life will assuage it, lays siege to his kingdom. Some of the unexpected loot she has carried away still embarrasses her. Not a little, however, is of such undeniable advantage that she may fairly contend that its capture alone justifies her campaign.

Go to-day into many a woman's club house, into many a drawing-room or studio at, let us say, the afternoon tea hour, and what will you see? One or probably more women in mannish suits and boots calmly smoking cigarettes while they talk, and talk well, about things in which women are not supposed to be interested, but which it is apparent they understand.

Look the exhibit over. It is made, you at once recognize, by women of character, position, and sense. They have simply found certain masculine ways to their liking and adopted them. The probability is that if anybody should object to their habits, many of them would be as bewildered as are the great majority of Americans by the demonstration that "nice" women can smoke and think nothing of it!

The cigarette, the boot, and much of the talk are only by-products of the woman's invasion of the man's world. She did not set out to win these spoils. They came to her in the campaign!

The objects of her attack were things she considered more fundamental. She was dissatisfied with the way her brain was being trained, her time employed, her influence directed. "Give us the man's way," was her demand, "then we shall understand real things, can fill our days with important tasks, will count as human beings."

There was no uncertainty in her notion of how this was to be accomplished. A woman rarely feels uncertainty about methods. She instinctively sees a way and follows it with assurance. Half her irritation against man has always been that he is a spendthrift with time and talk. Madame Roland, sitting at her sewing table listening to the excited debate of the Revolutionists in her salon, mourned that though the ideas were many, the resulting measures were few. It is the woman's eternal complaint against discussion--nothing comes of it. In a country like our own, where reflection usually follows action, the woman's natural mental attitude is exaggerated. It is one reason why we have so few houses where there is anything like conversation, why with us the salon as an institution is out of question. The woman wants immediately to incorporate her ideas. She is not interested in turning them over, letting her mind play with them. She has no patience with other points of view than her own. They are _wrong_--therefore why consider them? She detests uncertainties-- questions which cannot be settled. Only by man and the rare woman is it accepted that talk is a good enough end in itself.

The strength of woman's attack on man's life, apart from the essential soundness of the impulse which drove her to make it, lay then in its directness and practicality. She began by asking to be educated in the same way that man educated himself. Preferably she would enter his classroom, or if that was denied her, she would follow the "just-as-good" curriculum of the college founded for her. In the last sixty or seventy years tens of thousands of women have been students in American universities, colleges, and technical schools, taking there the same training as men. In the last twenty years the annual crescendo of numbers has been amazing; over ten thousand at the beginning of the period, over fifty-two thousand at the end. Over eight thousand degrees were given to women in 1910, nearly half as many as were given to men. Fully four fifths of these women students and graduates have worked side by side with men in schools which served both equally.

Here, then, is a great mass of experience from which it would seem that we ought to be able to say precisely how the intellects of the two sexes act and react under the stimulus of serious study, to decide definitely whether their attack on problems is the same, whether they come out the same. Nevertheless, he would be a rash observer who would pretend to lay down hard-and-fast generalizations. Assert whatever you will as to the mind of woman at work and some unimpeachable authority will rise up with experience that contradicts you. But the same may be said of the mind of man. The mind--_per se_--is a variable and disconcerting organ.

But admitting all this--certain generalizations, on the whole correct, may be made from our experience with coeducation.

One of the first of these is that at the start the woman takes her work more seriously than her masculine competitor. Fifty years ago there was special reason for this. The few who in those early days sought a man's education had something of the spirit of pioneers. They had set themselves a lofty task: to prove themselves the equal of man--to win privileges which they believed were maliciously denied their sex. The spirit with which they attacked their studies was illumined by the loftiness of their aim. The girl who enters college nowadays has rarely the opportunity to be either pioneer or martyr. She is doing what has come to be regarded as a matter of course. Nevertheless, to-day as then, in the coeducational institution she is more consciously on her mettle than the man.

Her attention, interest, respectfulness, docility, will be ahead of his. It will at once be apparent that she carries the larger stock of untaught knowledge. In the classroom she will usually outstep him in mathematics. It is an ideal subject for her, satisfying her talent for order, for making things "come out right." Her memory will serve her better. She can depend upon it to carry more exceptions to rules, more fantastic irregular verbs, more dates, more lists of kings and queens, battles and generals, and on the whole she will treat this sort of impedimenta with more respect. She will know less of abstract ideas, of philosophies and speculations. They will interest her less. The chances are that she will be less skillful with microscope and scalpel, though this is not certain. She will show less enthusiasm for technical problems, for machinery and engineering; more for social problems, particularly when it is a question of meeting them with preventives or remedies. In the first two or three years after entering college, she will almost invariably appear superior to the men of her age, more grown up, more interested, surer of herself, readier. Later you will find her on the whole less inclined to experiment with her gifts, to feel her wings, to make unexpected dashes into life. It begins to look as if he were the experimenter, she the conservator. And by the time she is a senior, look out! The chances are she will have less interest from now on with man's business and more with her own! In any case she will rarely develop as rapidly in his field from this point as he is doing.

He becomes assertive, confident, dominating; the male taking a male's place. He discovers that his intellectual processes are more scientific than hers, therefore he concludes they are superior. He finds he can outargue her, draw logical conclusions as she cannot. He can do anything with her but convince her, for she jumps the process, lands on her conclusion, and there she sits. Things are so because they are so. And the chances are she is right, in spite of the irregular way she got there. Something superior to reason enters into her operations--an intuition of truth akin to inspiration. In early ages women unusually endowed with this quality of perception were honored as seers. To-day they are recognized as counselors of prophetic wisdom. "If I had taken my wife's advice!" How often one hears it!

One most important fact has come out of our great coeducational experiment: The college cannot entirely rub feminity out and masculinity into a woman's brain. The woman's mind is still the woman's mind, although she is usually the last to recognize it. It is another proof of the eternal fact that Nature looks after her own good works!

But it takes more than a college course to make an efficient, flexible, and trustworthy organ from a mind, masculine or feminine. It must be applied to productive labor in competition with other trained minds, before you can decide what it is worth. Set the man-trained woman's mind at what is called man's business, let it be what you will--keeping a shop, practicing medicine or law, editing, running a factory--let her do it in what she considers to be a man's way, and with fidelity to her original theory that his way is more desirable than hers; that is, let her succeed in the task of making a man of herself--what about her?--what kind of a man does she become?

Here again there is ample experience to go on. For seventy years we have had them with us--the stern disciples of the militant program. Greater fidelity to a task than they show it would be impossible to find--a fidelity so unwavering that it is often painful. Their care for detail, for order, for exactness, is endless. Dignity, respect for their undertaking, devotion to professional etiquette they may be counted on to show in the highest degree. These are admirable qualities. They have led hundreds of women into independence and good service. Almost never, however, have they led one to the top. In free fields such as merchandising, editing, and manufacturing we have yet to produce a woman of the first caliber; that is, daring, experimenting, free from prejudice, with a vision of the future great enough to lead her to embody something of the future in her task.

In every profession we have scores of successful women--almost never a great woman, and yet the world is full of great women! That is, of women who understand, are familiar with the big sacrifices, appreciative of the fine things, far-seeing, prophetic. Why does this greatness so rarely find expression in their professional undertakings?

The answer is no doubt complex, but one factor is the general notion of the woman that if she succeeds she must suppress her natural emotions and meet the world with a surface as non-resilient as she conceives that of man to be in his dealings with the world. She is strengthened in this notion by hard necessity. No woman could live and respond as freely as her nature prompts to the calls on her sympathy which come in the contact with all conditions of life involved in practicing a trade or a profession. She must save herself. To do it she incases herself in an unnatural armor. For the normal, healthy woman this means the suppression of what is strongest in her nature, that power which differentiates her chiefly from man, her power of emotion, her "affectability" as the scientists call it. She must overcome her own nature, put it in bonds, cripple it, if she is to do her work. Here is a fundamental reason for the failure of woman to reach the first rank. She has sacrificed the most wonderful part of her endowment, that which when trained gives her vision, sharpens her intuitions, reveals the need and the true course. This superior affectability crushed, leaves her atrophied.

The common characterization of this atrophied woman is that she is "cold." It is the exact word. She is cold, also she is self-centered and intensely personal. Let a woman make success in a trade or profession her exclusive and sufficient ambition, and the result, though it may be brilliant, is repellent.

She gives to her task an altogether disproportionate place in her scheme of things. Life is not made by work, important as is work in life. Human nature has varied needs. It calls imperatively for a task, something to do with brain and hands--a productive something which fits the common good, without which the world would not be as orderly and as happy. Say what we will, it matters very little what the task is--if it contributes in some fashion to this superior orderliness and happiness. But it means more. It means leisure, pleasure, excitements; it means feeding of the taste, the curiosity, the emotions, the reflective powers; and it means love, love of the mate, the child, the friend, and neighbor. It means reverence for the scheme of things and one's place in it; worship of the author of it, religion.

But the woman sternly set to do a man's business, believing it better than the woman's, too often views life as made up of business. She throws her whole nature to the task. Her work is her child. She gives it the same exclusive passionate attention. She is as fiercely jealous of interference in it as she would be if it were a child. She resents suggestions and change. It is hers, a personal thing to which she clings as if it were a living being. That attitude is the chief reason why working with women in the development of great undertakings is as difficult as co 鮨 erating with them in the rearing of a family. It is also a reason why they rarely rise to the first rank. They cannot get away from their undertakings sufficiently to see the big truths and movements which are always impersonal.

Brilliant and satisfying as her triumph may be to her personally, she frequently finds that it is resented by nature and by society. She finds that nature lays pitfalls for her, cracks the ice of her heart and sets it aflame, often for absurd and unworthy causes. She finds that the great mass of unconscious women commiserate or scorn her as one who has missed the fullness of life. She finds that society regards her as one who shirked the task of life, and who, therefore, should not be honored as the woman who has stood up to the common burden. When she senses this--which is not always--she treats it as prejudice. As a matter of fact, the antagonism of Nature and Society to the militant woman is less prejudice than self-defense. It is a protest against the wastefulness and sacrifice of her career. It is a right saving impulse to prevent perversion of the qualities and powers of women which are most needed in the world, those qualities and powers which differentiate her from man, which make for the variety, the fullness, the charm, and interest of life.

Moreover, Nature and Society must not permit her triumph to appear desirable to the young. They must be made to understand what her winnings have cost in lovely and desirable things. They must know that the unrest which drove her to the attempt is not necessarily satisfied by her triumph, that it is merely stifled and may break out at any time in vagaries and follies. They must be made to realize the essential barrenness of her triumph, its lack of the savor and tang of life, the multitude of makeshifts she must practice to recompense her for the lack of the great adventure of natural living.

And they see it, many of them, before they are out of college, and their militancy falls off like the cloak it generally is. The girl abandons her quest. In the early days she was likely to be treated as an apostate if, instead of following the "life work" she had picked out, she slipped back into matrimony. I can remember the dismay among certain militant friends when Alice Freeman married. "Our first college president," they groaned. "A woman who so vindicated the sex." It was like the grieving of Miss Anthony that Mrs. Stanton wasted so much time having babies!

The militant theory, as originally conceived, instead of increasing in favor, has declined. There is little likelihood now that any great number of women will ever regard it as a desirable working formula for more than a short period of their lives. But I am not saying that this theory is no longer influential. It is probable that in a modified form it was never more influential than it is to-day. For, while the Uneasy Woman has practically demonstrated that "making a man of herself" does not solve her problem, she has by no means given up the notion that the Business of Being a Woman is narrowing and unsatisfying. Nor has she ceased to consider man's life more desirable than woman's.

The present effort of the serious-minded to meet the case takes two general directions, natural enough outgrowths of the original militancy. The first of these is a frank advocacy of celibacy. "Celibacy is the aristocracy of the future," is the preaching of one European feminist. It is a modification of the scheme by which the medieval woman sought to escape unrest. Four hundred years ago a woman sought celibacy as an escape from sin; service and righteousness were her aim. To-day she adopts it to escape inferiority and servitude; superiority and freedom her aim.

The ranks of the woman celibates are not full. Many a candidate falls out by the way, confronted by something she had not reckoned with--the eternal command that she be a woman. She compromises--grudgingly. She will be a woman on condition that she is guaranteed economic freedom, opportunity for self-expressive work, political recognition. What this amounts to is that she does not see in the woman's life a satisfying and permanent end. There are various points at which she claims it fails. It is antagonistic to personal ambition. It makes a dependent of her. It leaves her in middle life without an occupation. It keeps her out of the great movements of her day--gives her no part in the solution of the ethical and economical problems which affect her and her children. She declares that she wants fuller participation in life, and by life she seems to mean the elaborate machinery by which human wants are supplied and human beings kept in something like order; the movements of the market place, of politics, and of government.

Now if there were not something in her contention, the Uneasy Woman would not be with us as she is to-day, more vociferous, more insistent than ever in the world's history. What is there in her case?

If the cultivation of individual tastes and talents to a useful, productive point is out of question in the woman's business, if it is not a part of it, something is weak in the scheme. Something is weak if the woman is or feels that she is not paying her way. Both are not only individual rights; they are individual duties.

Moreover, she is certainly right to be dissatisfied, if, after spending twenty-five years, more or less, she is to be left in middle life, her forces spent, without interests and obligations which will occupy brain and heart to the full, without important tasks which are the logical outcome of her experience and which she must carry on in order to complete that experience.

But what is the truth about it? What is the Business of Being a Woman? Is it something incompatible with free and joyous development of one's talents? Is there no place in it for economic independence? Has it no essential relation to the world's movements? Is it an episode which drains the forces and leaves a dreary wreck behind? Is it something that cannot be organized into a profession of dignity, and opportunity for service and for happiness?

CHAPTER III

THE BUSINESS OF BEING A WOMAN

Respect for the Creator of this world is basic among all civilized people. The longer one lives, the more thoroughly one realizes the soundness of this respect. The earth and its works are good. Most human conceptions are barred by strange inconsistencies. The man who praises the works of the Creator as all wise not infrequently treats His arrangement for carrying on the race as if it were unfit to be spoken of in polite society. Nowhere does the modern God-fearing man come nearer to sacrilege than in his attitude toward the divine plan for renewing life.

A strange mixture of sincerity and hypocrisy, self-flagellation and lust, aspiration and superstition, has gone into the making of this attitude. With the development of it we have nothing to do here. What does concern us is the effect of this profanity on the Business of Being a Woman.

The central fact of the woman's life--Nature's reason for her--is the child, his bearing and rearing. There is no escape from the divine order that her life must be built around this constraint, duty, or privilege, as she may please to consider it. But from the beginning to the end of life she is never permitted to treat it naturally and frankly. As a child accepting all that opens to her as a matter of course, she is steered away from it as if it were something evil. Her first essays at evasion and spying often come to her in connection with facts which are sacred and beautiful and which she is perfectly willing to accept as such if they were treated intelligently and reverently. If she could be kept from all knowledge of the procession of new life except as Nature reveals it to her, there would be reason in her treatment. But this is impossible. From babyhood she breathes the atmosphere of unnatural prejudices and misconceptions which envelop the fact.

Throughout her girlhood the atmosphere grows thicker. She finally faces the most perilous and beautiful of experiences with little more than the ideas which have come to her from the confidences of evil-minded servants, inquisitive and imaginative playmates, or the gossip she overhears in her mother's society. Every other matter of her life, serious and commonplace, has received careful attention, but here she has been obliged to feel her way and, worst of abominations, to feel it with an inner fear that she ought not to know or seek to know.

If there were no other reason for the modern woman's revolt against marriage, the usual attitude toward its central facts would be sufficient. The idea that celibacy for woman is "the aristocracy of the future" is soundly based if the Business of Being a Woman rests on a mystery so questionable that it cannot be frankly and truthfully explained by a girl's mother at the moment her interest and curiosity seeks satisfaction. That she gets on as well as she does, results, of course, from the essential soundness of the girl's nature, the armor of modesty, right instinct, and reverence with which she is endowed.

The direst result of ignorance or of distorted ideas of this tremendous matter of carrying on human life is that it leaves the girl unconscious of the supreme importance of her mate. So heedlessly and ignorantly is our mating done to-day that the huge machinery of Church and State and the tremendous power of public opinion combined have been insufficient to preserve to the institution of marriage anything like the stability it once had, or that it is desirable that it should have, if its full possibilities are to be realized. The immorality and inhumanity of compelling the obviously mismated to live together, grow on society. Divorce and separation are more and more tolerated. Yet little is done to prevent the hasty and ill-considered mating which is at the source of the trouble.

Rarely has a girl a sound and informed sense to guide her in accepting her companion. The corollary of this bad proposition is that she has no sufficient idea of the seriousness of her undertaking. She starts out as if on a lifelong joyous holiday, primarily devised for her personal happiness. And what is happiness in her mind? Certainly it is not a good to be conquered--a state of mind wrested from life by tackling and mastering its varied experiences, the end, not the beginning, of a great journey. Too often it is that of the modern Uneasy Woman--the attainment of something outside of herself. She visualizes it, as possessions, as ease, a "good time," opportunities for self-culture, the exclusive devotion of the mate to her. Rarely does she understand that happiness in her undertaking depends upon the wisdom and sense with which she conquers a succession of hard places--calling for readjustment of her ideas and sacrifice of her desires. All this she must discover for herself. She is like a voyager who starts out on a great sea with no other chart than a sailor's yarns, no other compass than curiosity.

The budget of axioms she brings to her guidance she has picked up helter-skelter. They are the crumbs gathered from the table of the Uneasy Woman, or worse, of the pharisaical and satisfied woman, from good and bad books, from newspaper exploitations of divorce and scandal, from sly gossip with girls whose budget of marital wisdom is as higgledy-piggledy as her own.

And a pathetically trivial budget it is:--

"He must tell her everything." "He must always pick up what she drops." "He must dress for dinner." "He must remember her birthday." That is, she begins her adventure with a set of hard-and-fast rules,--and nothing in this life causes more mischief than the effort to force upon another one's own rules!

That marriage gives the finest opportunity that life affords for practicing, not rules, but principles, she has never been taught. Flexibility, adaptation, fair-mindedness, the habit of supplementing the weakness of the one by the strength of the other, all the fine things upon which the beauty, durability, and growth of human relations depend,--these are what decide the future of her marriage. These she misses while she insists on her rules; and ruin is often the end. Study the causes back of divorces and separations, the brutal criminal causes aside, and one finds that usually they begin in trivial things,-- an irritating habit or an offensive opinion persisted in on the one side and not endured philosophically on the other; a petty selfishness indulged on the one side and not accepted humorously on the other,--that is, the marriage is made or unmade by small, not great, things.

It is a lack of any serious consideration of the nature of the undertaking she is going into which permits her at the start to accept a false notion of her economic position. She agrees that she is being "supported"; she consents to accept what is given her; she even consents to ask for money. Men and society at large take her at her own valuation. Loose thinking by those who seek to influence public opinion has aggravated the trouble. They start with the idea that she is a parasite--does not pay her way. "Men hunt, fish, keep the cattle, or raise corn," says a popular writer, "for women to eat the game, the fish, the meat, and the corn." The inference is that the men alone render useful service. But neither man nor woman eats of these things until the woman has prepared them. The theory that the man who raises corn does a more important piece of work than the woman who makes it into bread is absurd. The theory that she does something more difficult and less interesting is equally absurd.

The practice of handing over the pay envelope at the end of the week to the woman, so common among laboring people, is a recognition of her equal economic function. It is a recognition that the venture of the two is common and that its success depends as much on the care and intelligence with which she spends the money as it does on the energy and steadiness with which he earns it. Whenever one or the other fails, trouble begins. The failure to understand this business side of the marriage relation almost inevitably produces humiliation and irritation. So serious has the strain become because of this false start that various devices have been suggested to repair it--Mr. Wells' "Paid Motherhood" is one; weekly wages as for a servant is another. Both notions encourage the primary mistake that the woman has not an equal economic place with the man in the marriage.

Marriage is a business as well as a sentimental partnership. But a business partnership brings grave practical responsibilities, and this, under our present system, the girl is rarely trained to face. She becomes a partner in an undertaking where her function is spending. The probability is she does not know a credit from a debit, has to learn to make out a check correctly, and has no conscience about the fundamental matter of living within the allowance which can be set aside for the family expenses. When this is true of her, she at once puts herself into the rank of an incompetent--she becomes an economic dependent. She has laid the foundation for becoming an Uneasy Woman.

It is common enough to hear women arguing that this close grappling with household economy is narrowing, not worthy of them. Why keeping track of the cost of eggs and butter and calculating how much your income will allow you to buy is any more narrowing than keeping track of the cost and quality of cotton or wool or iron and calculating how much a mill requires, it is hard to see. It is the same kind of a problem. Moreover, it has the added interest of being always an independent personal problem. Most men work under the deadening effect of impersonal routine. They do that which others have planned and for results in which they have no permanent share.

But the woman argues that her task has no relation to the state. Her failure to see that relation costs this country heavily. Her concern is with retail prices. If she does her work intelligently, she follows and studies every fluctuation of price in standards. She also knows whether she is receiving the proper quality and quantity; and yet so poorly have women discharged these obligations that dealers for years have been able to manipulate prices practically to please themselves, and as for quality and quantity we have the scandal of American woolen goods, of food adulteration, of false weights and measures. No one of these things could have come about in this country if woman had taken her business as a consumer with anything like the seriousness with which man takes his as a producer.

Her ignorance in handling the products of industry has helped the monopolistically inclined trust enormously. I can remember the day when the Beef Trust invaded a certain Middle Western town. The war on the old-time butchers of the village was open. "Buy of us," was the order, "or we'll fill the storage house so full that the legs of the steers will hang out of the windows, and we'll give away the meat." The women of the town had a prosperous club which might have resisted the tyranny which the members all deplored, but the club was busy that winter with the study of the Greek drama! They deplored the tyranny, but they bought the cut-rate meat--the old butchers fought to a finish, and the housekeepers are now paying higher prices for poorer meat and railing at the impotency of man in breaking up the Beef Trust!

If two years ago when the question of a higher duty on hosiery was before Congress any woman or club of women had come forward with carefully tabulated experiments, showing exactly the changes which have gone on of late years in the shape, color, and wearing quality of the 15-, 25-, and 50-cent stockings, the stockings of the poor, she would have rendered a genuine economic service. The women held mass meetings and prepared petitions instead, using on the one side the information the shopkeepers furnished, on the other that which the stocking manufacturers furnished. Agitation based upon anything but personal knowlledge is not a public service. It may be easily a grave public danger. The facts needed for fixing the hosiery duty the women should have furnished, for they buy the stockings.

If the Uneasy American Woman were really fulfilling her economic functions to-day, she would never allow a short pound of butter, a yard of adulterated woolen goods, to come into her home. She would never buy a ready-made garment which did not bear the label of the Consumer's League. She would recognize that she is a guardian of quality, honesty, and humanity in industry.

A persistent misconception of the nature and the possibilities of this practical side of the Business of Being a Woman runs through all present-day discussions of the changes in household economy. The woman no longer has a chance to pay her way, we are told, because it is really cheaper to buy bread than to bake it, to buy jam than to put it up. Of course, this is a part of the vicious notion that a woman only makes an economic return by the manual labor she does. The Uneasy Woman takes up the point and complains that she has nothing to do. But this release from certain kinds of labor once necessary, merely puts upon her the obligation to apply the ingenuity and imagination necessary to make her business meet the changes of an ever changing world. Because the conditions under which a household must be run now are not what they were fifty years ago is no proof that the woman no longer has here an important field of labor. There is more to the practical side of her business than preparing food for the family! It means, for one thing, the directing of its wants. The success of a household lies largely in its power of selection. To-day selection has given way to accumulation. The family becomes too often an incorporated company for getting things--with frightful results. The woman holds the only strong strategic position from which to war on this tendency, as well as on the habits of wastefulness which are making our national life increasingly hard and ugly. She is so positioned that she can cultivate and enforce simplicity and thrift, the two habits which make most for elegance and for satisfaction in the material things of life.

Whenever a woman does master this economic side of her business in a manner worthy of its importance, she establishes the most effective school for teaching thrift, quality, management, selection--all the factors in the economic problem. Such scientific household management is the rarest kind of a training school. And here we touch the most vital part in the Woman's Business--that of education.

Every home is perforce a good or bad educational center. It does its work in spite of every effort to shirk or supplement it. No teacher can entirely undo what it does, be that good or bad. The natural joyous opening of a child's mind depends on its first intimate relations. These are, as a rule, with the mother. It is the mother who "takes an interest," who oftenest decides whether the new mind shall open frankly and fearlessly. How she does her work, depends less upon her ability to answer questions than her effort not to discourage them; less upon her ability to lead authoritatively into great fields than her efforts to push the child ahead into those which attract him. To be responsive to his interests is the woman's greatest contribution to the child's development.

I remember a call once made on me by two little girls when our time was spent in an excited discussion of the parts of speech. They were living facts to them, as real as if their discovery had been printed that morning for the first time in the newspaper. I was interested to find who it was that had been able to keep their minds so naturally alive. I found that it came from the family habit of treating with respect whatever each child turned up. Nothing was slurred over as if it had no relation to life--not even the parts of speech! They were not asked or forced to load themselves up with baggage in which they soon discovered their parents had no interest. Everything was treated as if it had a permanent place in the scheme to which they were being introduced. It is only in some such relation that the natural bent of most children can flower, that they can come early to themselves. Where this warming, nourishing intimacy is wanting, where the child is turned over to schools to be put through the mass drill which numbers make imperative--it is impossible for the most intelligent teacher to do a great deal to help the child to his own. What the Uneasy Woman forgets is that no two children born were ever alike, and no two children who grow to manhood and womanhood will ever live the same life. The effort to make one child like another, to make him what his parents want, not what he is born to be, is one of the most cruel and wasteful in society. It is the woman's business to prevent this.

The Uneasy Woman tells you that this close attention to the child is too confining, too narrowing. "I will pity Mrs. Jones for the hugeness of her task," says Chesterton; "I will never pity her for its smallness." A woman never lived who did all she might have done to open the mind of her child for its great adventure. It is an exhaustless task. The woman who sees it knows she has need of all the education the college can give, all the experience and culture she can gather. She knows that the fuller her individual life, the broader her interests, the better for the child. She should be a person in his eyes. The real service of the "higher education," the freedom to take a part in whatever interests or stimulates her--lies in the fact that it fits her intellectually to be a companion worthy of a child. She should know that unless she does this thing for him he goes forth with his mind still in swaddling clothes, with the chances that it will not be released until relentless life tears off the bands.

The progress of society depends upon getting out of men and women an increasing amount of the powers with which they are born and which bad surroundings at the start blunt or stupefy. This is what all systems of education try to do, but the result of all systems of education depends upon the material that comes to the educator. Opening the mind of the child, that is the delicate task the state asks of the mother, and the quality of the future state depends upon the way she discharges this part of her business.

I think it is historically correct to say that the reason of the sudden and revolutionary change in the education of American women, which began with the nineteenth century and continued through it, was the realization that if we were to make real democrats, we must begin with the child, and if we began with the child, we must begin with the mother!

Everybody saw that unless the child learned by example and precept the great principles of liberty, equality, and fraternity, he was going to remain what by nature we all are,--imperious, demanding, and self-seeking. The whole scheme must fail if his education failed. It is not too much to say that the success of the Declaration of Independence and the Constitution depended, in the minds of certain early Democrats, upon the woman. The doctrines of these great instruments would be worked out according to the way she played her part. Her serious responsibility came in the fact that her work was one that nobody could take off her hands. This responsibility required a preparation entirely different from that which had been hers. She must be given education and liberty. The woman saw this, and the story of her efforts to secure both, that she might meet the requirements, is one of the noblest in history. There was no doubt, then, as to the value of the tasks, no question as to their being worthy national obligations. It was a question of fitting herself for them.

But what has happened? In the process of preparing herself to discharge more adequately her task as a woman in a republic, her respect for the task has been weakened. In this process, which we call emancipation, she has in a sense lost sight of the purposes of emancipation. Interested in acquiring new tools, she has come to believe the tools more important than the thing for which she was to use them. She has found out that with education and freedom, pursuits of all sorts are open to her, and by following these pursuits she can preserve her personal liberty, avoid the grave responsibility, the almost inevitable sorrows and anxieties, which belong to family life. She can choose her friends and change them. She can travel, and gratify her tastes, satisfy her personal ambitions. The snare has been too great; the beauty and joy of free individual life have dulled the sober sense of national obligation. The result is that she is frequently failing to discharge satisfactorily some of the most imperative demands the nation makes upon her.

Take as an illustration the moral training of the child. The most essential obligation in a Woman's Business is establishing her household on a sound moral basis. If a child is anchored to basic principles, it is because his home is built on them. If he understands integrity as a man, it is usually because a woman has done her work well. If she has not done it well, it is probable that he will be a disturbance and a menace when he is turned over to society. Sending defective steel to a gunmaker is no more certain to result in unsafe guns than turning out boys who are shifty and tricky is to result in a corrupt and unhappy community.

Appalled by the seriousness of the task, or lured from it by the joys of liberty and education, the woman has too generally shifted it to other shoulders--

shoulders which were waiting to help her work out the problem, but which could never be a substitute. She has turned over the child to the teacher, secular and religious, and fancied that he might be made a man of integrity by an elaborate system of teaching in a mass. Has this shifting of responsibility no relation to the general lowering of our commercial and political morality?

For years we have been bombarded with evidence of an appalling indifference to the moral quality of our commercial and political transactions. It is not too much to say that the revelations of corruption in our American cities, the use of town councils, State legislatures, and even of the Federal Government in the interests of private business, have discredited the democratic system throughout the world. It has given more material for those of other lands who despise democracy to sneer at us than anything that has yet happened in this land. And _this has come about under the r 閒 ime of the emancipated woman_. Is she in no way responsible for it? If she had kept the early ideals of the woman's part in democracy as clearly before her eyes as she has kept some of her personal wants and needs, could there have been so disastrous a condition? Would she be the Uneasy Woman she is if she had kept faith with the ideals that forced her emancipation?--if she had not substituted for them dreams of personal ambition, happiness, and freedom!

The failure to fulfill your function in the scheme under which you live always produces unrest. Content of mind is usually in proportion to the service one renders in an undertaking he believes worth while. If our Uneasy Woman could grasp the full meaning of her place in this democracy, a place so essential that democracy must be overthrown unless she rises to it--a part which man is not equipped to play and which he ought not to be asked to play, would she not cease to apologize for herself--cease to look with envy on man's occupations? Would she not rise to her part and we not have at last the "new woman" of whom we have talked so long?

Learning, business careers, political and industrial activities--none of these things is more than incidental in the national task of woman. Her great task is to prepare the citizen. The citizen is not prepared by a training in practical politics. Something more fundamental is required. The meaning of honor and of the sanctity of one's word, the understanding of the principles of democracy and of the society in which we live, the love of humanity, and the desire to serve,--these are what make a good citizen. The tools for preparing herself to give this training are in the woman's hands. It calls for education, and the nation has provided it. It calls for freedom of movement and expression, and she has them. It calls for ability to organize, to discuss problems, to work for whatever changes are essential. She is developing this ability. It may be that it calls for the vote. I do not myself see this, but it is certain that she will have the vote as soon as not a majority, but an approximate half, not of men--but of women--feel the need of it.

What she has partially at least lost sight of is that education, freedom, organization, agitation, the suffrage, are but tools to an end. What she now needs is to formulate that end so nobly and clearly that the most ignorant woman may understand it. The failure to do this is leading her deeper and deeper into fruitless unrest. It is also dulling her sense of the necessity of keeping her business abreast with the times. At one particular and vital point this shows painfully, and that is her slowness in socializing her home.

CHAPTER IV

THE SOCIALIZATION OF THE HOME

It is only by much junketing about that one comes to the full realization of what men and women in the main are doing in this country. One learns as he passes from town to town, through cities and across plains, that the general reason for industry everywhere is to get the means to build and support a home. Row upon row, street upon street, they run in every village you traverse. They dot the hills and valleys, they break up the mountain side.

Every night they draw to their shelter millions of men who have toiled since morning to earn the money to build and keep them running. All day they shelter millions of women who toil from dawn to dark to put meaning into them. To shelter two people and the children that come to them, to provide them a place in which to eat and sleep, is that the only function of these homes? If that were all, few homes would be built. When that becomes all, the home is no more! To furnish a body for a soul, that is the physical function of the home.

There are certain people who cry out that for a woman this undertaking has no meaning--that for her it is a cook stove and a dustpan, a childbed, and a man who regards her as his servant. One might with equal justice say that for the man it is made up of ten, twelve, or more hours, at the plow, the engine, the counter, or the pen for the sake of supporting a woman and children whom he rarely sees! Unhappily, there are such combinations; they are not homes! They are deplorable failures of people who have tried to make homes. To insist that they are anything else is to overlook the facts of life, to doubt the sanity of mankind which hopefully and courageously goes on building, building, building, sacrificing, binding itself forever and ever to what?--a shell? No, to the institution which its observation and experience tell it, is the one out of which men and women have gotten the most hope, dignity, and joy,-- the place through which, whatever its failures and illusions, they get the fullest development and the opportunity to render the most useful social service.

It is this grounded conviction that the home takes first rank among social institutions which gives its tremendous seriousness to the Business of Being a Woman. She is the one who must sit always at its center, the one who holds a strategic position for dealing directly with its problems. Far from these problems being purely of a menial nature, as some would have us believe, they are of the most delicate social and spiritual import. A woman in reality is at the head of a social laboratory where all the problems are of primary, not secondary, importance, since they all deal directly with human life.

One of the most illuminating experiences of travel is visiting the great chateaux of France. One goes to see "historical monuments," the scenes of strange and tragic human experiences; he finds he is in somebody's private house, which by order of the government is opened to the public one day of the week! He probably will not realize this fully unless he suddenly opens a door, not intended to be opened, behind which he finds a mass of children's toys--go-carts and dolls, balls and tennis rackets--or stumbles into a room supposed to be locked where framed photographs, sofa cushions, and sewing tables abound!

To the average American it comes almost as a shock that these open homes are the logic of democracy. It is almost sure to set him thinking that after all the home, anybody's home, even one in such big contrast to this chateau as a two-story frame house, on Avenue A, in B-ville, has a relation to the public. He has touched a great social truth.

To socialize her home, that is the high undertaking a woman has on her hands if she is to get at the heart of her Business. And what do we mean by socialization? Is it other than to put the stamp of affectionate, intelligent human interest upon all the operations and the intercourse of the center she directs? To make a place in which the various members can live freely and draw to themselves those with whom they are sympathetic--a place in which there is spiritual and intellectual room for all to grow and be happy each in his own way?

I doubt if there is any problem in the Woman's Business which requires a higher grade of intelligence, and certainly none that requires broader sympathies, than this of giving to her home that quality of stimulation and joyousness which makes young and old seek it gladly and freely.

To do this requires money, freedom, time, and strength? No, what I mean does not depend upon these things. It is the notion that it does that often prevents its growth. For it is a spirit, an attitude of mind, and not a formula or a piece of machinery. As far as my observation goes it is quite, if not more likely, to be found in a three-room apartment, where a family is living on fifteen dollars a week, as in an East Central Park mansion! In these little families where love prevails--it usually does exist. It is the kind of an atmosphere in which a man prefers to smoke his pipe rather than go to the saloon; where the girl brings her young man home rather than walk with him. Mutual interest and affection is its note. Such homes do exist by the tens of thousands; even in New York City. It is not from them that girls go to brothels or boys to the Tombs.

Externally, these homes are often pretty bad to look at--overcrowded, disorderly, and noisy. Cleanliness, order, and space are good things, but it is a mistake to think that there is no virtue without them. There are more primary and essential things; things to which they should be added, but without which they are lifeless virtues. In one of Miss Loane's reports on the life of the English poor, she makes these truthful observations:--

One learns to understand how it is that the dirty, untidy young wife, who, when her husband returns hungry and tired from a long day's work, holds up a smilingly assured face to be kissed, exclaiming, "Gracious! if I hadn't forgot all about your tea!" and clatters together an extravagant and ill-chosen meal while she pours out a stream of cheerful and inconsequent chatter, is more loved, and dealt with more patiently, tenderly, and faithfully, than her clean and frugal neighbor, who has prepared a meal that ought to turn the author of Twenty Satisfying Suppers for Sixpence green with envy, but who expects her husband to be eternally grateful because "he could eat his dinner off the boards,"--when all that the poor man asks is to be allowed to walk over them unreproached.

Peace and good will may go with disorder and carelessness! They may fly order and thrift. They will fly them when order and thrift are held as the more desirable. A woman is often slow to learn that good housekeeping alone cannot produce a milieu in which family happiness thrives and to which people naturally gravitate. She looks at it as the fulfillment of the law--the end of her Business. It is the exaggerated place she gives it in the scheme of things, which brings disaster to her happiness and gives substance to the argument that woman's lot in life is fatal to her development. Housekeeping is only the shell of a Woman's Business. Women lose themselves in it as men lose themselves in shopkeeping, farming, editing. Knowing nothing but your work is one of the commonest human mistakes. Pitifully enough it is often a deliberate mistake--the only way or the easiest way one finds to quiet an unsatisfied heart. The undue place given good housekeeping in many a woman's scheme of life is the more tragic because it is a distortion of one of the finest things in the human experience--the satisfaction of doing a thing well. It is a satisfaction which the worker must have if he is to get joy from his labor. But labor is not for the sake of itself. It must have its human reason. You rejoice in a "deep-driven plow"--but if there was to be no harvest, your straight, full furrows would be little comfort. You rejoice to build a stanch and beautiful house, but if you knew it was to stand forever vacant, joy would go from your task. An end work must have. One does not keep house for its own sake. It is absorption in the process--the refusal to allow it to be forgotten or utilized freely, that makes the work barren. It is like becoming so absorbed in a beautiful frame that you are unconscious of the picture--unconscious that there is a picture. Things must serve their purpose if they are to convince of their beauty. Try living in a room with a wonderfully fitted fireplace; its mantel of exquisite design and workmanship, its fire irons masterpieces of art--and no heat from it! Note how utterly distasteful it all becomes. It is no longer beautiful because it does not do the work it was made beautiful to do.

One of the most repellent houses in which I have ever visited was one in which there was, from garret to cellar, so far as I discovered, not one article which was not of the period imitated, not one streak of color which was not "right." It was a masterpiece of correct furnishing, but it gave one a curious sense of limitation. One could not escape the scheme. The inelasticity of it hampered sociability--and there grew on one, too, a sense of unfitness. His clothes were an anachronism! They were the only thing which did not belong!

There is an old-fashioned adjective which describes better than any other this preoccupation with things, which so often prevents a woman's coming to an understanding of the heart of her Business. It is old maidish. It has often been the pathetic fate of single women to live alone. To minister to themselves becomes their occupation. The force of their natures turns to their belongings. If in straitened circumstances they give their souls to spotless floors; if rich, to flawless mahogany and china, to perfect household machinery. Wherever you find in woman this perversion--old maidish is perhaps the most accurate word for her--it is a sacrifice of the human to the material. A house without sweet human litter, without the trace of many varying tastes and occupations, without the trail of friends who perhaps have no sense of beauty but who love to give, without the scars of use, and the dust of running feet--what is it but a meatless shell!

This devotion to "things" may easily become a ghoulish passion. It is such that Ibsen hints at in the Master Builder, when he makes Aline Solness attribute her perpetual black, her somber eyes and smileless lips, not to the death of her two little boys which has come about through the burning of her home, that was a "dispensation of Providence" to which she "bows in submission," but to the destruction of the things which were "mine"--"All the old portraits were burnt upon the walls, and all the old silk dresses were burnt that had belonged to the family for generations and generations. And all mother's and grandmother's lace--that was burnt, too, and only think, the jewels too."

One of the most disastrous effects of this preocccupation with the things and the labors of the household is the killing of conversation. There is perhaps no more general weakness in the average American family than glumness! The silent newspaper-reading father, the worried watchful mother, the surly boy, the fretful girl, these are characters typical in both town and country. In one of Mrs. Daskam Bacon's lively tales, "Ardelia in Arcadia," the little heroine is transplanted from a lively, chattering, sweltering New York street to the maddening silence of an overworked farmer's table. She stands it as long as she can, then cries out, "For Gawd's sake, talk!"

One secret of the attraction for the young of the city over the country or small town is contact with those who talk. They are conscious of the exercise of a freedom they have never known--the freedom to say what rises to the lips. They experience the unknown joy of play of mind. According to their observation the tongue and mind are used only when needed for serious service: to keep them active, to allow them to perform whatever nimble feats their owners fancy--this is a revelation!

Free family talk is sometimes ruined by a mistaken effort to direct it according to some artificial notions of what conversation means. Conversation means free giving of what is uppermost in the mind. The more spontaneous it is the more interesting and genuine it is. It is this freedom which gives to the talk of the child its surprises and often its startling power to set one thinking. Holding talk to some severe standard of consistency, dignity, or subject is sure to stiffen and hamper it. There could have been nothing very free or joyful about talking according to a program as the ladies of the eighteenth-century salons were more or less inclined. Good conversation runs like water; nothing is foreign to it. "Farming is such an unintellectual subject," I heard a critical young woman say to her husband, whose tastes were bucolic. The young woman did not realize that one of the masterpieces of the greatest of the world's writers was on farming--most practical farming, too! That which relates to the life of each, interests each, concerns each--that is the material for conversation, if it is to be enjoyable or productive.

One of a woman's real difficulties in creating a free-speaking household is her natural tendency to regard opinions as personal. To differ is something she finds it difficult to tolerate. To her mind it is to be unfriendly. This propensity to give a personal turn to things is an expression of that intensity of nature which makes her, as Mr. Kipling has truthfully put it, "more deadly than the male!" She must be that--were she not, the race would dwindle. He would never sacrifice himself as she does for the preservation of the young! This necessity of concentrating her whole being on a little group makes her personal. The wise woman is she who recognizes that like all great forces this, too, has its weakness. Because a woman must be "more deadly than the male" in watching her offspring is no reason she should be so in guarding an opinion. Certainly if she is so, conversation is cut off at the root.

Not infrequently she is loath to encourage free expression because it seems to her to disturb the peace. Certainly it does disturb fixity of views. It does prevent things becoming settled in the way that the woman, as a rule, loves to have them, but this disturbance prevents the rigid intellectual and spiritual atmosphere which often drives the young from home. Peace which comes from submission and restraint is a poor thing. In the long run it turns to revolt. The woman, if she examines her own soul, knows the effect upon it of habitual submission to a husband's opinion. She knows it is a habit fatal to her own development. While at the beginning she may have been willing enough to sacrifice her ideas, later she makes the painful discovery that this hostage to love, as she considered it, has only made her less interesting, less important, both to herself and to him. It has made it the more difficult, also, to work out that socialization of her home which, as her children grow older, she realizes, if she thinks, is one of her most imperative duties.

A woman is very prone to look on marriage as a merger of personalities, but there can be no great union where an individuality permits itself to be ruined. The notion that a woman's happiness depends on the man--that he must "make her happy"--is a basic untruth. Life is an individual problem, and consequently happiness must be. Others may hamper it, but in the final summing up it is you, not another, who gives or takes it--no two people can work out a high relation if the precious inner self of either is sacrificed.

Emerson has said the great word:--

Leave all for love; _Yet, hear me, yet, Keep thee to-day, To-morrow, forever, Free as an Arab! Of thy beloved_.

The "open house," that is, the socialized house, depends upon this free mind to a degree only second to that spirit of "good will to man," upon which it certainly must, like all institutions in a democratic Christian nation, be based. This good will is only another name for neighborliness--the spirit of friendly recognition of all those who come within one's radius. Neighborliness is based upon the Christian and democratic proposition that all men are brothers--a proposition with which the sects and parties of Christianity and democracy often play havoc. In their zeal for an interpretation or system they sacrifice the very things they were devised to perpetuate and extend among men. A sectarian or partisan household cannot be a genuinely neighborly household. It has cut off too large a part of its source of supply.

The most perfect type of this spirit of neighborliness which we have worked out in this country, outside of the thousands of little homes where it exists and of which, in the nature of the case, only those who have felt their influence can know, is undoubtedly Hull House, the Chicago Settlement under the direction of Jane Addams. Hull House is an "open house" for its neighborhood. It is a place where men and women of all ages, conditions, and points of view are welcome. So far as I have been able to discover, genuine freedom of mind and friendliness of spirit are what have made Hull House possible and are what will decide its future after the day of the great woman who has mothered it and about whom it revolves. There is no formula for building a Hull House--any more than there is a home. Both are the florescence of a spirit and a mind. Each will form itself according to the ideas, the tastes, and the cultivation of the individuality at its center. Its activities will follow the peculiar needs which she has the brains and heart to discover, the ingenuity and energy to meet.

Hull House serves its neighborhood, and in so doing it serves most fully its own household. Its own members are the ones whose minds get the most illumination from its activities. Moreover, Hull House from its first-hand sympathetic dealing with men and women in its neighborhood learns the needs of the neighborhood. It is and for years has been a constant source of suggestion and of agitation for the betterment of the conditions under which its neighbors--and indirectly the whole city, even nation--live and work. Health, mind, morals, all are in its care. It is practical in the plans it offers. It can back up its demands with knowledge founded on actual contact. It can rally all of the enlightened and decent forces of the city to its help. Hull House, indeed, is a very source of pure life in the great city where it belongs.

So far as attitude of mind and spirit go, the home should be to the little neighborhood in which it works what Hull House is to its great field. In its essential structure it is the same thing; _i.e._ Hull House is really modeled after the home. Most interesting is the parallel between its organization and its activities and those of many a great home which we know through the lives of their mistresses, that of Margaret Winthrop, of Eliza Pinckney, of Mrs. John Adams.

The social significance of Hull House is in its relative degree the possible social significance of every home in this land. The realization depends entirely upon the conception the woman in a particular house has of this side of her Business--whether or no she sees neighborliness in this big sense. That she does not see it is too often due to the fact that even though she may have "gone through college," she has no notion of society as a living structure made up of various interdependent institutions, the first and foremost of which is a family or home.

Absurd as it is, Society, which is founded on the family, is to-day giving only perfunctory and half-hearted attention to the family. The whole vocabulary of the institution has taken on such a quality of cant, that one almost hesitates to use the words "home" and "mother"! A girl's education should contain at least as much serious instruction on the relation of the family to Society as it does on the relation of the Carboniferous Age to the making of the globe. At present, it usually has less. It is but another evidence of the pressing need there is of giving to the Woman's Business a more scientific treatment--of revitalizing its vocabulary, reformulating its problems, of giving it the dignity it deserves, that of a great profession. It is the failure to do this which is at the bottom of woman's present disorderly and antisocial handling of three of the leading occupations of her life--her clothes, her domestics, and her daughter.

CHAPTER V

A WOMAN AND HER RAIMENT

One of the most domineering impulses in men and women is that bidding them to make themselves beautiful. In the normal girl-child it comes out, as does her craving for a doll. Nature is telling her what her work in the world is to be. It stays with her to the end, its flame often flickering long after her arms have ceased their desire to cradle a child. Scorn it, ridicule it, deny it, it is nature's will, and as such must be obeyed, and in the obeying should be honored.

But this instinct, which has led men and women from strings of shells to modern clothes, like every other human instinct, has its distortions. It is in the failure to see the relative importance of things, to keep the proportions, that human beings lose control of their endowment. Give an instinct an inch, and it invariably takes its ell! The instinct for clothes, from which we have learned so much in our climb from savagery, has more than once had the upper hand of us. So dangerous to the prosperity and the seriousness of peoples has its tyranny been, that laws have again and again been passed to check it; punishments have been devised to frighten off men from indulging it; whole classes have been put into dull and formless costumes to crucify it.

Man gradually and in the main has conquered his passion for ornament. To-day, in the leading nations of the world, he clothes rather than arrays himself. Woman has not harnessed the instinct. She still allows it to drive her, and often to her own grave prejudice. Even in a democracy like our own, woman has not been able to master this problem of clothes. In fact, democracy has complicated the problem seriously.

Under the old r 間 ime costumes had been worked out for the various classes. They were adapted both to the purse and to the pursuit. They were fitting--that is, silk was not worn in huts or homespun in palaces; slippers were for carriages and sabots for streets. The garments of a class were founded on good sound principles on the whole--but they marked the class. Democracy sought to destroy outward distinctions. The proscribed costumes went into the pot with proscribed positions. Under democracy we can cook in silk petticoats and go to the White House in a cap and apron, if we will. And we often will, that being a way to advertise our equality!

Class costumes destroyed, the principles back of them, that is, fitness, quality, responsibility, were forgotten. The old instinct for ornament broke loose. Its tyranny was strengthened by the eternal desire of the individual to prove himself superior to his fellows. Wealth is the generally accepted standard of measurement of value in this country to-day, and there is no way in which the average man can show wealth so clearly as in encouraging his women folk to array themselves. Thus we have the anomaly in a democracy of a primitive instinct let loose, and the adoption of discarded aristocratic devices for proving you are better than your neighbor, at least in the one revered particular of having more money to spend!

The complication of the woman's life by this domination of clothes is extremely serious. In many cases it becomes not one of the sides of her business, but the business of her life. Such undue proportion has the matter taken in the American Woman's life under democracy that one is sometimes inclined to wonder if it is not the real "woman question." Certainly in numbers of cases it is the rock upon which a family's happiness splits. The point is not at all that women should not occupy themselves seriously with dress, that they should not look on it as an art, as legitimate as any other. The difficulty comes in not mastering the art, in the entirely disproportionate amount of attention which is given to the subject, in the disregard of sound principles.

The economic side of the matter presses hard on the whole country. It is not too much to say that the chief economic concern of a great body of women is how to get money to dress, not as they should, but as they want to. It is to get money for clothes that drives many, though of course not the majority, of girls, into shops, factories, and offices. It is because they are using all they earn on themselves that they are able to make the brave showing that they do. Many a girl is misjudged by the well-meaning observer or investigator because of this fact--"She could never dress like that on $6, $8, or $15 a week and support herself," they tell you. She does not support herself. She works for clothes, and clothes alone. Moreover, the girl who has the pluck to do hard regular work that she may dress better has interest enough to work at night to make her earnings go farther. No one who has been thrown much with office girls but knows case after case of girls who with the aid of some older member of the family cut and make their gowns, plan and trim their hats. Moreover, this relieving the family budget of dressing the girl is a boon to fathers and mothers.

It is hard on industry, however, for the wage earner who can afford to take $6 or $8 helps pull down the wages of other thousands who support not only themselves, but others.

Moreover, to put in one's days in hard labor simply to dress well, for that is the amount of it, is demoralizing. It is this emphasis on the matter which impels a reckless girl sometimes to sell herself for money to buy clothes. "I wanted the money," I heard a girl, arrested for her first street soliciting, tell the judge. "Had you no home?" "Yes." "A good home?" "Yes." "For what did you want money?" "Clothes."

"Gee, but I felt as if I would give anything for one of them willow plumes," a pretty sixteen-year-old girl told the police matron who had rescued her from a man with whom she had left home, because he promised her silk gowns and hats with feathers.

This ugly preoccupation with dress does not begin with the bottom of society. It exists there because it exists at the top and filters down. In each successive layer there are women to whom dress is as much of a vice as it was for the poor little girls I quote above. It is a vice curiously parallel to that of gambling among men. Women of great wealth not infrequently spend princely allowances and then run accounts which come into the courts by their inability or unwillingness to pay them. It is curious comment on women in a democracy that it should be possible to mention them in the same breath with Josephine, Empress of the French. Napoleon at the beginning of the Empire allowed Josephine $72,000 a year for her toilet; later he made it $90,000. But there was never a year she did not far outstrip the allowance. Masson declares that on an average she spent $220,000 a year, and the itemized accounts of the articles in her wardrobe give authority for the amount.

Josephine's case is of course exceptional in history. She was an untrained woman, generous and pleasure-loving, utterly without a sense of responsibility. She had all the instincts and habits of a demi-mondaine; moreover, she had been thrust into a position where she was expected to live up to traditions of great magnificence. Her passion for ornament had every temptation and excuse, for it was constantly excited by the hoards of greedy tradesmen and of no less greedy ladies-in-waiting who hung about her urging her to buy and give. It is hard to believe that Josephine's case could be even remotely suggested in our democracy; yet one woman in American society bought last summer in Europe a half-dozen nightgowns for which she paid a thousand dollars apiece. There are women who will start on a journey with a hundred or a hundred and fifty pairs of shoes. There are others who bring back from Europe forty or fifty new gowns for a season! What can one think of a bill of $500 for stockings in one season, of $20,000 for a season's gowns, coats and hats from one shop and as much more in the aggregate for the same articles in the same period from other shops; this showing was made in a recent divorce case.

What can one think of duties of over $30,000 paid on personal articles by one woman who yearly brings back similar quantities of jewelry and clothes. This $30,000 in duties meant an expenditure of probably about $100,000. It included over $1200 for hats, over $3000 for corsets and lingerie. This was undoubtedly exceptional; that is, few women of even great wealth buy so lavishly. Yet good round sums, even if they are small in comparison, are spent by many women in their European outings. They will bring from six to twelve gowns which will average at least $150 apiece, and an occasional woman will have a half-dozen averaging from $450 to $500 apiece. One might say that eight to twelve hats, costing $25 to $50 apiece, was a fair average, though $800 to $1200 worth is not so rare as to cause a panic at the customhouse.

The comparative amounts which men and women spend affords an interesting comment on the relative importance which men and women attach to clothes. In one case of which I happen to know Mr. A. brought in $840 worth of wearing apparel: Mrs. A. nearly $10,000 worth, of which $7000 was for gowns. A man may have eight to ten suits of pajamas which cost him $10 apiece, a dozen or two waistcoats, a dozen or two shirts, a few dozen handkerchiefs and gloves, a dozen or so ties, eight or ten suits of clothes, but from $500 to $1000 will cover his wardrobe; his wife will often spend as much for hats alone as he does for an entire outfit!

The difficulty in these great expenditures is that they set a pace. To many women of wealth they are no doubt revolting. They recognize that there are only two classes of women who can justify them--the actress and the demi-mondaine. Yet insensibly many of these women yield to the pressure of temptation. The influence is subtle, often unconscious, and for this reason spreads the more widely. Women all over the country find that the pressure is to spend more for clothes each year. The standard changes. Occasions multiply. Fantasies entice. Before they know it their clothes are costing them a disproportionate sum--more than they can afford if their budget is to balance.

This does not apply to one class, it creeps steadily down to the very poor. Investigators of small household budgets lay it down as a rule that as the income increases the percentage spent for clothing increases more rapidly than for any other item. It is true in the professional classes, and especially burdensome there; for the income is usually small, but the social demand great.

There are certain industrial and ethical results from this preoccupation with clothes which should not be overlooked, particularly the indifference to quality which it has engendered. The very heart of the question of clothes of the American woman is imitation. That is, we are not engaged in an effort to work out individuality. We are not engaged in an effort to find costumes which by their expression of the taste and the spirit of this people can be fixed upon as appropriate American costumes, something of our own. From top to bottom we are copying. The woman of wealth goes to Paris and Vienna for the real masterpieces in a season's wardrobe. The great dressmakers and milliners go to the same cities for their models. Those who cannot go abroad to seek inspiration and ideas copy those who have gone or the fashion plates they import. The French or Viennese mode, started on upper Fifth Avenue, spreads to 23d St., from 23d St. to 14th St., from 14th St. to Grand and Canal. Each move sees it reproduced in materials a little less elegant and durable, its colors a trifle vulgarized, its ornaments cheapened, its laces poorer. By the time it reaches Grand Street the $400 gown in brocaded velvet from the best looms in Europe has become a cotton velvet from Lawrence or Fall River, decorated with mercerized lace and glass ornaments from Rhode Island! A travesty--and yet a recognizable travesty. The East Side hovers over it as Fifth Avenue has done over the original. The very shop window, where it is displayed, is dressed and painted and lighted in imitation of the uptown shop. The same process goes on inland. This same gown will travel its downward path from New York westward, until the Grand St. creation arrives in some cheap and gay mining or factory town. From start to finish it is imitation, and on this imitation vast industries are built--imitations of silk, of velvet, of lace, of jewels.

These imitations, cheap as they are, are a far greater extravagance, for their buyers, than the original model was for its buyer, for the latter came from that class where money does not count--while the former is of a class where every penny counts. The pity of it is that the young girls, who put all that they earn into elaborate lingerie at seventy-nine cents a set (the original model probably sold at $50 or $100), into open-work hose at twenty-five cents a pair (the original $10 a pair), into willow plumes at $1.19 (the original sold at $50), never have a durable or suitable garment. They are bravely ornamented, but never properly clothed. Moreover, they are brave but for a day. Their purchases have no goodness in them; they tear, grow rusty, fall to pieces with the first few wearings, and the poor little victims are shabby and bedraggled often before they have paid for their belongings, for many of these things are bought on the installment plan, particularly hats and gowns. Under these circumstances, it is little wonder that one hears, often and often among their class, the bitter cry, "Gee, but it's hell to be poor!"--that one finds so often assigned by a girl as the cause of her downfall, the natural reason--"Wanted to dress like other girls"--"Wanted pretty clothes."

This habit of buying poor imitations does not end in the girl's life with her clothes. When she marries, she carries it into her home. Decoration, not furnishing, is the keynote of all she touches. It is she who is the best patron of the elaborate and monstrous cheap furniture, rugs, draperies, crockery, bric-a-brac, which fill the shops of the cheaper quarters of the great cities, and usually all quarters of the newer inland towns.

Has all this no relation to national prosperity--to the cost of living? The effect on the victim's personal budget is clear--the effect it has on the family budget, which it dominates, is clear. In both cases nothing of permanent value is acquired. The good linen undergarments, the "all wool" gown, the broadcloth cape or coat, those standard garments which the thrifty once acquired and cherished, only awaken the mirth of the pretty little spendthrift on $8 a week. Solid pieces of furniture such as often dignify even the huts of European peasants and are passed down from mother to daughter for generations--are objects of contempt by the younger generation here. Even the daughters of good old New England farmers are found to-day glad to exchange mahogany for quartered oak and English pewter for pressed glass and stamped crockery. True, another generation may come in and buy it all back at fabulous prices, but the waste of it!

This production of shoddy cloth, cotton laces, cheap furniture, what is it but waste! Waste of labor and material! Time and money and strength which might have been turned to producing things of permanent values, have been spent in things which have no goodness in them, things which because of their lack of integrity and soundness must be forever duplicated, instead of freeing industry to go ahead, producing other good and permanent things.

What it all amounts to is that the instinct for ornament has gotten the upper hand of a great body of American women. We have failed so far to develop standards of taste, fitness, and quality, strong, sure, and good enough effectually to impose themselves. There is no national taste in dress; there is only admirable skill in adapting fashions made in other countries. There is no national sense of restraint and proportion. It is pretty generally agreed that getting all you can is entirely justifiable. There is no national sense of quality; even the rich to-day in this country wear imitation laces. The effect of all this is a bewildering restlessness in costume--a sheeplike willingness to follow to the extreme the grotesque and the fantastic. The very general adoption of the ugly and meaningless fashions of the last few years--peach-basket hats, hobble skirts, slippers for the street--is a case in point. From every side this is bad--defeating its own purpose--corrupting national taste and wasting national substance.

Moreover, the false standard it sets up socially is intolerable. It sounds fantastic to say that whole bodies of women place their chief reliance for social advancement on dress, but it is true. They are, or are not, as they are gowned! The worst of this fantasy is not only that it forces too much attention from useful women, but that it gives such poise and assurance to the ignorant and useless! If you look like the women of a set, you are as "good" as they, is the democratic standard of many a young woman. If for any reason she is not able to produce this effect, she shrinks from contact, whatever her talent or charm! And she is often not altogether wrong in thinking she will not be welcome if her dress is not that of the circle to which she aspires. Many a woman indifferently gowned has been made to feel her difference from the elegant she found herself among. If she is sure of herself and has a sense of humor, this may be an amusing experience. To many, however, it is an embittering one!

Now these observations are not presented as discoveries! They were true, at least, as far back as the Greeks. In fact, there is nothing in the so-called woman's movement, which in its essence did not exist then. The stream of human aspirations, with its stretches of wisdom and of folly, has flowed steadily through the ages, and on its troubled surface men and women have always struggled together as they are struggling to-day. These little comments simply seem to the writer worth making because for the moment the truths behind them are not getting as much attention as they deserve. Certainly the tyranny dress exercises over the woman in this American democracy is an old enough theme. Indeed, it has always formed a part of her program of emancipation. Out of her revolt against its absurdities has come the most definite development in American costume which we have had, and that is the sensible street costume, which in spite of efforts to distort and displace it, a woman still may wear without differentiating herself from her fellows.

The short skirt and jacket, the shirt waist and stout boots, a woman is allowed to-day, are among the good things which the Woman's Rights movement of the 40's and 50's helped secure for us. When those able leaders made their attack on man, demanding that the world in which he moved be opened to them, they were quick enough to see that if they succeeded in their undertaking they would be hampered by their clothes. They revolted! True, they did not voice this revolt in their historic list of "injuries and usurpations on the part of man toward woman." They did not say, "He has compelled her to hamper herself with skirts and stays, to decorate her head with rats and puffs, to paint her face with poisonous compounds, to walk the street in footwear which is neither suitable nor comfortable!"

This statement, however, would have had the same quality of truth as several which were included in the "List of Grievances"; the same as the declaration: "He has compelled her to submit to laws in the formation of which she has had no voice," or, "He has denied her the facilities for obtaining a thorough education, all colleges being closed against her."

Dress reformers were admitted to the ranks of the agitators. The initial revolt was thoroughgoing. They discarded the corset, discarded it when it was still improper to speak the word! They cut off their hair, cut it off in a day when every woman owned a chignon. They discarded the corset, cut off their hair, and adopted bloomers!

The story of the bloomer is piquant. It was launched and worn. It became the subject of platform oratory and had its organ. Why is it not worn to-day? No woman who has ever masqueraded in man's dress or donned it for climbing will ever forget the freedom of it. Yet the only woman in the Christian world who ever wore it at once naturally and with that touch of coquetry which is necessary to carry it off, as far as this writer's personal observation goes, was Madame Dieulafoy, and Madame Dieulafoy was protected by the French government and an exclusive circle.

Bloomers proved too much for even the courage of dear Miss Anthony. For two years she wore them, and then with tears and lamentations resigned them. In that resignation Miss Anthony paid tribute, unconsciously no doubt, to something deeper than she ever grasped in the woman question. Her valiant soul met its master in her own nature, but she did not recognize it. She abandoned her convenient and becoming costume because of prejudice, she said. What other prejudice ever dismayed her! She thrived on fighting them; she met her woman's soul, and did not know it!

But from the experiments and blunders and travail of some of these noble and early militants over the dress question, has come, as I have said, our present useful, and probably permanent type of street suit. In this particular the American woman has achieved a genuine democratization of her clothes. The experience of the last two years--fashion's open attempt to make the walking suit useless by tightening the skirts, and bizarre by elaborate decorations, has in the main failed. Here, then, is a standard established, and established on one of the great principles of sensible clothing, and that is fitness. It shows that the true attack on the tyranny and corruption of clothes lies in the establishment of principles.

These principles are, briefly:--

The fitness of dress depends upon the occasion.

The beauty of dress depends upon line and color.

The ethics of dress depends upon quality and the relation of cost to one's means.

In time we may get into the heads of all women, rich and poor, that an open-work stocking and low shoe for winter street wear are as unfit as they all concede a trailing skirt to be. In time we may even hope to train the eye until it recognizes the difference between a beautiful and a grotesque form, between a flowing and a jagged line. In time we may restore the sense of quality, which our grandmothers certainly had, and which almost every European peasant brings with her to this country.

These principles are teachable things. Let her once grasp them and the vagaries of style will become as distasteful as poor drawing does to one whose eye has learned what is correct, as lying is to one who has cultivated the taste for the truth.

Martha Berry tells of an illuminating experience in her school of Southern mountain girls. She had taken great pains to teach them correct standards and principles of dress. She had been careful to see that simplicity and quality and fitness were all that they saw in the dress of their teachers. Then one day they had visitors, fashionable visitors, in hobble skirts and strange hats and jingling with many ornaments. They were good and interesting women, and they talked sympathetically and well to the girls. Miss Berry was crushed. "What will the girls think of my teachings?" she asked herself. "They will believe I do not know." But that night one of her assistants said to her: "I have just overheard the girls discussing our visitors. They liked them so much, but they are saying that it is such a pity that they could not have had you to teach them how to dress."

As a method of education, instruction in the principles of dress is admirable for a girl. Through it she can be made to grasp the truth which women so generally suspect to-day; that is, the _importance of the common and universal things of life_; the fact that all these everyday processes are the expressions of the great underlying truths of life. A girl can be taught, too, through this matter of dress, as directly perhaps as through anything that concerns her, the importance of studying human follies! Follies grow out of powerful human instincts, ineradicable elements of human nature. They would not exist if there were not at the bottom of them some impulse of nature, right and beautiful and essential. The folly of woman's dress lies not in her instinct to make herself beautiful, it lies in her ignorance of the principles of beauty, of the intimate and essential connection between utility and beauty. It lies in the pitiful assumption that she can achieve her end by imitation, that she can be the thing she envies if she look like that thing.

The matter of dress is the more important, because bound up with it is a whole grist of social and economic problems. It is part and parcel of the problem of the cost of living, of woman's wages, of wasteful industries, of the social evil itself. It is a woman's most direct weapon against industrial abuses, her all-powerful weapon as a consumer. At the time of the Lawrence strike, Miss Vida Scudder, of Wellesley College, is reported to have said in a talk to a group of women citizens in Lawrence:--

"I speak for thousands besides myself when I say that I would rather never again wear a thread of woolen than know my garments had been woven at the cost of such misery as I have seen and known, past the shadow of a doubt, to have existed in this town."

Miss Scudder might have been more emphatic and still have been entirely within the limit of plain obligation; she might have said, "I will never again wear a thread of woolen woven at the cost of such misery as exists in this town." Women will not be doing their duty, as citizens in this country, until they recognize fully the obligations laid upon them by their control of consumption.

The very heart of the question of the dress is, then, economic and social. It is one of those great everyday matters on which the moral and physical well-being of society rests. One of those matters, which, rightly understood, fill the everyday life with big meanings, show it related to every great movement for the betterment of man.

Like all of the great interests in the Business of Being a Woman, it is primarily an individual problem, and every woman who solves it for herself, that is, arrives at what may be called a sound mode of dress, makes a real contribution to society. There is a tendency to overlook the value of the individual solution of the problems of life, and yet, the successful individual solution is perhaps the most genuine and fundamental contribution a man or woman can make. The end of living is a life--fair, sound, sweet, complete. The vast machinery of life to which we give so much attention, our governments and societies, our politics and wrangling, is nothing in itself. It is only a series of contrivances to insure the chance to grow a life. He who proves that he can conquer his conditions, can adjust himself to the machinery in which he finds himself, he is the most genuine of social servants. He realizes the thing for which we talk and scheme, and so proves that our dreams are not vain!

CHAPTER VI

THE WOMAN AND DEMOCRACY

The one notion that democracy has succeeded in planting firmly in the mind of the average American citizen is his right and duty to rise in the world. Tested by this conception the American woman is an ideal democrat. Give her a ghost of a chance and she almost never fails to better herself materially and socially. Nor can she be said to do it by the clumsy methods we describe as "pushing." She does it by a legitimate, if rather literal, application of the national formula for rising,--get schooling and get money.

The average American man reverses the order of the terms in the formula. He believes more in money. The time that boys and girls are kept in school after the fourteen-or sixteen-year-age limit is generally due to the insistence of the mother, her confidence that the more education, the better the life chance. What it amounts to is that the man has more faith in life as a teacher, the woman more faith in schools. Both, however, seek the same goal, pin their faith to the same tools. Both take it for granted that if they work out the formulas, they thereby earn and will receive letters patent to the aristocracy of the democracy!

The weakness of this popular conception of the democratic scheme is that it gives too much attention to what a man gets and too little to what he gives. Democracy more than any other scheme under which men have tried to live together depends on what each returns--returns not in material but in spiritual things. Democracy is not a shelter, a garment, a cash account; it is a spirit. The real test of its followers must be sought in their attitude of mind toward life, labor, and their fellows.

Where does the average American woman come out in applying this test? Take her attitude toward labor,--where does it place her? Labor according to democracy is a badge of respectability. You cannot poach or sponge in a democracy; if you do, you violate the fundamental right of the other man. You cannot ask him to help support you by indirect or concealed devices; if you do, you are hampering the free opportunity the scheme promises him.

Moreover, the kind of work you do must not demean you. Nothing useful is menial. It is in the quality of the work and the spirit you give it that the test lies. Poor work brings disrespect and so hurts not only you but the whole mass. Contempt for a task violates the principle because it is contempt for a thing which the system recognizes as useful. Classification based on tasks falls down in a democracy. A poor lawyer falls below a good clerk, a poor teacher below a good housemaid, since one renders a sound and the other an unsound service.

Now this ideal of labor it was for the woman to work out in the household. To do this she must reconstruct the ideas to which she and all her society had been trained. In the nature of the task there could be no rules for it. It could be accomplished only by creating in the household a genuine democratic spirit. This meant that she must bring herself to look upon domestic service as a dignified employment in no way demeaning the person who performed it. Quite as difficult, she must infuse into those who performed the labor of the household respect and pride in their service.

What has happened? Has the woman democratized the department of labor she controls? If we are to measure her understanding of the system under which she lives by what she has done with her own particular labor problem, we must set her down as a poor enough democrat. This great department of national activity is generally (though by no means universally) in a poorer estate to-day than ever before in the history of the country; that is, tested by the ideals of labor toward which we are supposed to be working, it shows less progress.

Instead of being dignified, it has been demeaned. No other honest work in the country so belittles a woman socially as housework performed for money. It is the only field of labor which has scarcely felt the touch of the modern labor movement; the only one where the hours, conditions, and wages are not being attacked generally; the only one in which there is no organization or standardization, no training, no regular road of progress. It is the only field of labor in which there seems to be a general tendency to abandon the democratic notion and return frankly to the standards of the aristocratic r 聞 ime. The multiplication of livery, the tipping system, the terms of address, all show an increasing imitation of the old world's methods. Unhappily enough, they are used with little or none of the old world's ease. Being imitations and not natural growths, they, of course, cannot be.

More serious still is the relation which has been shown to exist between criminality and household occupations. Nothing, indeed, which recent investigation has established ought to startle the American woman more. Contrary to public opinion, it is not the factory and shop which are making the greatest number of women offenders of all kinds; it is the household. In a recent careful study of over 3000 women criminals, the Bureau of Labor found that 80 per cent came directly from their own homes or from the traditional pursuits of women![2]

The anomaly is the more painful because women are so active in trying to better the conditions in trades which men control. Feminine circles everywhere have been convulsed with sympathy for shop and factory girls. Intelligent and persistent efforts are making to reach and aid them. This is, of course, right, and it would be a national calamity if such organizations as the Woman's Trade Union League and the Consumer's League should lose anything of their vigor. But the need of the classes they reach is really less than the need of household workers. In the first place, the number affected is far less.

It is customary, in presenting the case of the shop and factory girl, to speak of them as "an army 7,000,000 strong." It is a misleading exaggeration. The whole number of American women and girls over ten years of age earning their living wholly or partially is about 7,000,000.[3] Of this number from 20 per cent to 25 per cent belong to the "army" in shops and factories; moreover, a goodly percentage of this proportion are accountants, bookkeepers, and stenographers,--a class which on the whole may be said to be able to look after its own needs. The number in domestic service is nearly twice as great, something like 40 per cent of the 7,000,000.

There are almost as many dressmakers, milliners, and seamstresses as there are factory operators in this 7,000,000. There are nearly twice as many earning their living in dairies, greenhouses, and gardens as there are in shops and offices.

The greater number in domestic service is not what gives this class its greater importance. Its chief importance comes from the fact that it is in a permanent woman's employment; that is, the household worker becomes on marriage a housekeeper and in this country frequently an employer of labor. The intelligence and the ideals which she will give to her homemaking will depend almost entirely on what she has seen in the houses where she has worked; that is, our domestic service is _self-perpetuating_, and upon it American homes are in great numbers being annually founded. In sharp contrast to this permanent character of housework is the transientness of factory and shop work. The average period which a girl gives to this kind of labor is probably less than five years. What she learns has little or no relation to her future as a housekeeper--indeed, the tendency is rather to unfit than to fit her for a home.

But why is the American woman not stirred by these facts? Why does she not recognize their meaning and grapple with her labor problem? It is certain that at the beginning of the republic she did have a pretty clear idea of the kind of household revolution the country needed. Our great-grandmothers, that is, the serious ones among them, made a brave dash at it. There is no family, at least of New England tradition, who does not know the methods they adopted. They changed the nomenclature. There were to be no more "servants"--we were to have helpers. There were to be no divisions in the household. The helper was to sit at the table, at the fireside. (They thought to change the nature of a relation as old as the world by changing its name and form.) It was like the French Revolutionists' attempt to make a patriot by taking away his ruffles and shoe buckles and calling him "citizen"!

Of course it failed. The family meal, the fireside hour, are personal and private institutions in a home. Much of the success of the family in building up an intimate comradeship depends upon preserving them. We admit friends to them as a proof of affection, strangers as a proof of our regard. The notion that those who come into a household solely to aid in its labor should be admitted into personal relations which depend for their life upon privacy and affection, was always fantastic. It could not endure, because it violated something as important as the dignity of labor, and that was the sacredness of personal privacy. Moreover, it was bound to fail because it made the dignity of labor depend on artificial things--such as the name by which one is called, the place where one sits.

The good sense of the country might very well have regulated whatever was artificial in the attempt, if it had not been for the crushing interference of slavery. In the South all service was performed by slaves. In many parts of the North, at the founding of the republic, in Connecticut, in New York, New Jersey, slaves were held. It was practically impossible to work out a democratic system of domestic service side by side with this institution.

Slavery passed, but we were impeded by the fact that, liberated, the slave was still a slave in spirit and that his employer, North and South, was still an aristocrat in her treatment of him. With this situation to cope with, the woman's labor problem was still further complicated by immigration.

For years we have been overrun by thousands of untrained girls who are probably to be heads of American homes and mothers of American citizens. Most of them are of good, healthy, honest, industrious stock, but they are ignorant of our ways and ideas. The natural place for these girls to get their initiation into American democracy is in the American household. The duty of American women toward these foreign girls is plainly to help them understand our ideals. The difficulty of this is apparent; but the failure to accomplish it has been due less to its difficulty than to the fact that not one woman in a thousand has recognized that she has an obligation to make a fit citizen of the girl who comes into her home.

Generally speaking, the foreign servant girl has been exploited in this country almost if not quite as ruthlessly and unintelligently as the foreign factory girl and the foreign steel mill worker. Domestic service, which ought to be the best school for the newcomer, has become the worst; exploited, she learns to exploit; suspected, she learns to suspect. The result has been that the girl has soon acquired a confused and grotesque notion of her place. She soon becomes insolent and dissatisfied, grows more and more indifferent to the quality of her work and to the cultivation of right relations.

What we have lost in our treatment of the immigrant women can never be regained. We forget that almost invariably these girls have the habit of thrift.

They have never known anything else. Thrift as a principle is ingrained in them. But the American household is notoriously thriftless. As a rule it destroys the quality in the untrained immigrant girl. It is American not to care for expense--and she accepts the method--as far as her mistress' goods are concerned--if not her own.

The general stupid assumption that because the immigrant girl does not know our ways she knows nothing, has deprived us of much that she might have contributed to our domestic arts and sciences. It is with her as it is with any newcomer in a strange land of strange tongue--she is shy, dreads ridicule. Instead of encouraging her to preserve and develop that which she has learned at home, we drive her to abandon it by our ignorant assumption that she knows nothing worth our learning. The case of peasant handicraft is in point. It is only recently that we have begun to realize that most women immigrants know some kind of beautiful handicraft which they have entirely dropped for fear of being laughed at.

A very frequent excuse for the lack of pains that the average woman gives to the training of the raw girl is that she marries as soon as she becomes useful. But is it not part of the woman's business in this democracy to help the newcomer to an independent position? Is it not part of her business to help settle her servants in matrimony? Certainly any large and serious conception of her business must include this obligation.

It is the failure to recognize opportunities for public service of this kind that makes the woman say her life is narrow. It is parallel to her failure to understand the relation of household economy to national economy. She seems to lack the imagination to relate her problem to the whole problem. She will read books and follow lecture courses on Labor and come home to resent the narrowness of her life, unconscious that she personally has the labor problem on her own hands and that her failure to see that fact is complicating daily the problems of the nation. It is the old false idea that the interesting and important thing is somewhere else--never at home--while the truth is that the only interesting and important thing for any one of us is in mastering our own particular situation,--moreover, the only real contribution we ever make comes in doing that.

The failure to dignify and professionalize household labor is particularly hard on the unskilled girl of little education who respects herself, has pretty clear ideas of her "rights" under our system of government, and who expects to make something of herself. There are tens of thousands of such in the country; very many of them realize clearly the many advantages of household labor. They know that it ought to be more healthful, is better paid, is more interesting because more varied. They see its logical relation to the future to which they look forward.

But such a girl feels keenly the cost to herself of undertaking what she instinctively feels ought to be for her the better task. She knows the standards and conditions are a matter of chance; that, while she may receive considerate treatment in one place, in another there will be no apparent consciousness that she is a human being. She knows and dreads the loneliness of the average "place." "It's breaking my heart I was," sobbed an intelligent Irish girl, serving a term for drunkenness begun in the kitchen, "alone all day long with never a one to pass a good word." She finds herself cut off from most of the benefits which are provided for other wage-earning girls. She finds girls' clubhouses generally are closed to her. She is the pariah among workers.

What is there for this girl but the factory or the shop? Yet her presence there is a disaster for the whole labor system, for she is a _cheap laborer_-- cheap not because she is a poor laborer--she is not; generally she is an admirable one--quick to learn, faithful to discharge. Her weakness in trade is that she is a transient who takes no interest in fitting herself for an advanced position. The demonstration of this statement is found in a town like Fall River, where the admirable textile school has only a rare woman student, although boys and men tax its capacity. There is no object for the average girl to take the training. She looks forward to a different life. The working girl has still to be convinced of the "aristocracy of celibacy"!

No more difficult or important undertaking awaits the American woman than to accept the challenge to democratize her own special field of labor. It is in doing this that she is going to make her chief contribution to solving the problem of woman in industry. It is in doing this that she is going to learn the meaning of democracy. It is an undertaking in which every woman has a direct individual part--just as every man has a direct part in the democratization of public life.

Individual effort aside, though it is the most fundamental, she has various special channels of power through which she can work--her clubs, for instance. If the vast machinery of the Federation of Woman's Clubs could be turned to this problem of the democratization of domestic service, what an awakening might we not hope for! Yet it is doubtful if it will be through the trained woman's organizations that the needed revolution will come. It will come, as always, from the ranks of the workers.

Already there are signs that the woman's labor organizations are willing to recognize the inherent dignity of household service. And this is as it should be. The woman who labors should be the one to recognize that all labor is per se equally honorable--that there is no stigma in any honestly performed, useful service. If she is to bring to the labor world the regeneration she dreams, she must begin not by saying that the shop girl, the clerk, the teacher, are in a higher class than the cook, the waitress, the maid, but that we are all laborers alike, sisters by virtue of the service we are rendering society. That is, labor should be the last to recognize the canker of caste.[4]

FOOTNOTES:

[2] Report on Condition of Woman and Child Wage Earners in the United States, Vol. XV. Relation between Occupation and Criminality of Women. 1911.

[3] The number of people in 1910 in what is called "gainful occupations" has not as yet been compiled by the Census Bureau. This figure of 7,000,000 is arrived at by the following method, suggested to the writer by Director Durand. It is known that there are about 44,500,000 females in the present population. Now in 1900 there were about 14?per cent of all the girls and women in the country over ten years of age at work a part or all of the time. Apply to the new figure this proportion, and you have between six and seven millions, which is called 7,000,000 here, on the supposition that the proportion may have increased. The percentage of women in each of the various occupations in 1900 is assumed still to exist.

[4] The National Women's Trades Union League has domestic workers among its members, though not as yet, I believe, in any large numbers. Its

officials are strong believers in a Domestic Workers' Union. There are several such unions in New Zealand, and they have done much to regulate hours, conditions, and wages.

CHAPTER VII

THE HOMELESS DAUGHTER

One of the severest strains society makes on human life is that of adapting itself to ever changing conditions: yesterday it dragged us in a stagecoach; to-day it hurls us across country in limited expresses; to-morrow we shall fly! Once twilight and darkness were without, shadows and dim recesses within; now, wherever men gather there is one continuous blazing day. He who would keep his task abreast with the day must accept speed and light; for the law is, think, feel, do in the terms of your day, if you would keep your hold on your day.

It is a law often resented as if it were an immorality, but those who refuse the new way on principle, confuse form with principle. It is the form which changes, not the essence. The few great underlying elements from which character and happiness are evolved are permanent--their mutations are endless. Dull-minded, we take the mutations to mean shifting of principle. That is, we do not square up by truth, but by the forms of truth.

The Woman's Business has always suffered from lack of facility in adapting itself to new forms of expression. The natural task found, a method of handling it in a fashion sufficiently acceptable to prevent family revolts mastered, and the woman usually is as fixed as a star in its orbit. She resents changes of method, new interpretations, and fresh expressions. It is she, not man, who stands an immovable mountain in the path of militant feminism.

In this course she is following her nature. An instinct more powerful than logic tells her that she must preserve the thing she is making, that center for which she is responsible, that place where her child is born and reared, where her mate retreats, to be reassured that the effort to which he has committed himself is worth while, where all the community to which she belongs is served and strengthened. If this place is preserved, she must do it. Man, an experimenter and adventurer, cannot.

Changes she fears. She sees them as disturbers of her plans and her ideals. But the changes will not stay. They gather about her retreat, beat at the doors, creep in at the windows, win her husband and children from her very arms. The home on which she depended to keep them becomes impotent. While she stands an implacable guardian of a form of truth, truth has moved on, broadened its outlook, and clothed itself in new expressions.

It is entirely understandable that the woman who sees herself left behind with her dead gods should cry out against change as the ruin of her hopes. It is equally understandable that those who find themselves adrift should doubt the home as an institution. At the bottom of the revolt of thousands of our "uneasy women" of to-day lies this doubt. The home failed them, and with the logic of limited experience they cast it out of their calculations.

But the home is one of the unescapable facts of nature and society-- unescapable because the child demands it. One of the earliest convictions of the child is that he has a right to a home. To him it appears as the great necessity. He cannot see himself outside of it. To be at large in the world throws him into panic. The sacrifices and pains very young children suffer uncomplainingly, particularly in great cities and factory towns, is a pathetic enough demonstration of what the word means to them. Mere children by the hundreds support families terrified by the thought of their collapse. The orphan forever dreams of the day when a home will be found for him. The child whose parents seek freedom, leaving him to school or servants, never fails to nourish a sense of injustice. Whatever one generation may decide as to the futility or burdensomeness of the home, the oncoming child will force its return.

To keep this permanent place abreast with growing truth, that is the obligation of the woman. It is the failure to do this that produces what we may call the homeless daughter; that girl who loved and often served to the point of folly, finds herself in a group where none of the imperative needs the day has awakened in her are met.

One of the first of these needs is for what we call "economic independence." The spirit of our day and of our system of government is personal, material independence for all. Under the old r 閒 ime the girl had her economic place.

The family was a small community. It provided for most of its own wants, hence the girl must be taught household arts and science, all of the fine traditional knowledge and skill which made, not drudges, but skilled managers, skilled cooks and needlewomen, skilled hostesses and nurses. She had a business to learn under the old r 閒 ime, and there was an authority, often severely enforced no doubt, which made her learn it well. There was the same appraising of the efficiency of the girl for her business there was of the boy for his.

The girl of to-day rarely has any such systematic training for the material side of her business, nor is a dignified place provided for her in well-to-do families. Her place is parasitical and demoralizing. Take the young girl who has been what we call "educated"; that is, one who has gone through college and has not found a talent which she is eager to develop. The spirit of the times makes her less keen for marriage, puts no feeling of obligation of marriage upon her. She finds herself in a home which is not regarded as a serious industrial undertaking. Things go on more or less accidentally, according to traditions or conventions. Her ideas of scientific management, if she has any, are treated as revolutionary. Her help is not needed. There is no place for her.

The daughters of the very poor often have better fortune than she in this respect. They, from very early years, have known that they were necessary to the family. Almost invariably they accept heavy and sometimes cruel burdens cheerfully, even proudly. It is the pride of knowing themselves important to those whom they love. One of the difficult things to combat in enforcing the laws which forbid children under fourteen working, is the child's desire to help. He may hate the hardship, but at least there is in his lot none of that hopeless sense of futility which comes over the girl of high spirit when she realizes she has no practical value in the group to which she belongs. "Not needed"--that is one of the tragic experiences of the young girl in the well-to-do family. To save herself, to meet the truth of her day which has taken hold of her, she must seek a productive place; that is, leave home, seek work. If she has some special talent, knows what she wants to do, she is fortunate indeed. With the majority it is work, something to do, a place where they can be independently productive, that is sought.

The girl of the family in moderate circumstances is no better off. She must contribute in some way, and there is no scientific management in her home--no study of ways and means which enables her to contribute and remain at home. She is driven outside in order to support herself. I cannot but believe that here is one of the gravest weaknesses in our educational machinery, this failure to give the girl inclined to remain at home a training which would enable her to help make more of a limited income. Nothing is so rare to-day as the fine habit of making much of little. A dollar mixed with brains is worth five in every place where dollars are used. Particularly is this true in the household. The failure to teach how to mix brains and dollars, and to inspire respect for the undertaking, annually drives thousands of girls into our already overburdened industrial system who would be healthier and happier at home and who would render there a much greater economic service. Such work as is being done in certain Western agricultural colleges for girls, in the Carnegie School for Women in Pittsburg, in Miss Kittridge's Household Centers in New York City, is a recognition of this need of making scientific managers--trained household workers--of young women. There is no more practical way of relieving the industrial strain.

It is not always the dependent and so humiliating position a girl finds herself in that drives her from home. It is frequently the discovery that she is a member of a group that has no responsible place in the community; that regards itself as a purely isolated, unrelated, irresponsible unit,--an atom without affinities! The home can be, if it will, the most antisocial force in existence, for it can, if it will, exist practically for itself. That excessive individualism, which is responsible for so many evils in our country, has encouraged this isolation. The girl who finds herself without a productive place at home at the same time finds none of the fine inspiration which comes from fitting herself into a social scheme and helping to do its work. The spirit of the age is social. She feels its call, she sees how unresponsive, even antipathetic, to it her home is. She concludes that if she is to serve she must seek something to do in some remote city. The attraction the Social Settlement has for the girl finds its base here. The loss to communities of their educated young women, who find no response to their need, no place to serve in their own society, is incalculable.

It is not infrequent that a girl who may have by some chance of fortune a sufficient sense of independence in her home, who knows herself needed there, and is ready to perform the service, is driven out by the persistence of that spirit of parental authority, which looks upon it as a duty to rule the life, particularly of the daughter, as long as she is at home. There is nothing clearer than that the old domination of one person by another is a thing of the past. A new spirit of co 鮨 eration and friendly direction has come into the world. The home which it does not pervade cannot keep its young.

The most essential thing for a woman to understand is that her business is not to order her daughter's life, but to assist that daughter to shape it herself. She should be prepared to say to her: "The most interesting and important thing in the world for you is to work out your own particular life. You must build it from the place where you stand and with the materials in your hands. Nobody else ever stood in your particular place or ever will stand in one identical; nobody ever has or can possess the same materials. You alone can fuse the elements. Hold your place; do not try to shift into the place that another occupies. Keep your eye on what you have to work with, not on what somebody else has. The ultimate result, the originality, flavor, distinction, usefulness of your life, depend on the care, the reverence, and the intelligence with which you work up and out from where you are and with what you have."

It is only the woman who is prepared to say something like that to her daughter, to help her to see it, and to rise to it that has brought into her home the spirit of to-day.

Where there is failure at any one of these points, and if one fails, all probably will, since they are obvious elements in the liberal view of life, the girl must go forth if her life is to go progressively on. She must seek work, less for the sake of work than for the sake of life. To remain where she is, unproductive in a group which does not recognize the calls of the present world and where _another person_--for the mother who tries to force the individuality becomes another person--insists on shaping her course,--to do this is to quench the spirit, stop the very breath of life.

The girl goes forth to seek work. She has almost invariably the idea that work outside the home has less of drudgery in it, _i.e._ less routine and meanness, more excitement. She is unprepared for the years of steady grinding labor which she must go through to earn her bread in any trade or profession. She learns that work is work whether done in kitchen, sewing room, countinghouse, studio, or editor's sanctum, and all that keeps the operations which consume the bulk of the worker's time in any of these places from being drudgery is that he keeps before him the end for which they are performed. The first disillusionment comes, then, when she faces the necessity of a long steady pull for years if she is to "arrive."

A second comes when she finds she must prove to a busy, driven world that she is worth its attention; she must do more than simply knock for admission and declare her fealty to its ideals. She realizes sooner or later that she is an outsider and must delve her way in. No sapper works harder to make his trench than most young women do to make stable places for themselves in strange communities.

The gnawing loneliness of the girl who has left home to make her way is one of the most fruitful causes of the questionable relations which well-born girls form more often than society realizes. The girl seizes eagerly every chance for companionship or pleasure. Her keen need of it makes her overappreciative and undercritical. Moreover, she has the confidence of ignorance. Most American girls are brought up as if wrongdoing were impossible to them. Nobody has ever suggested to them that they have the possibility of all crimes in their makeup! Parents and teachers ordinarily have extraordinary skill in evading, but little in facing, the facts of life.

Disarmed by her ignorance, the girl goes out to a freedom such as no country has ever before believed it safe to allow the young, either girl or boy. This freedom is of course the logical result of what we call the "emancipation of women." It is the swinging of the pendulum from the old system of chaperonage and authority. The weak point is in the fact that the girl has not knowledge enough for her freedom. It is not a return of the old system of guarded girls which is needed. That is impossible under modern conditions, out of harmony with modern ideas. The great need is that the women of the country realize that freedom unaccompanied by knowledge is one of the most dangerous tools that can be put into a human being's hands. The reluctance of women to face this fact is the most discouraging side of the woman question.

The girl who goes forth should go armed with knowledge. Moreover, in moments of loneliness, when she is ready to slip, she should be literally jerked back by the pull of the home. This hold of the home is no chimerical thing. It is a positive, living reality. The home has a power of projecting itself into the lives of those who go out from it. It is where the girl does not carry away a sense of an uninterrupted relation--a certainty that she is a part of that group and that achievement, that she is only carrying on, enlarging, helping to extend, beautify, and ripen its work, that she is not homeless. Nothing can so hold her in her isolation as that sense.

The Uneasy Woman of to-day who has fulfilled to the letter, as she understands it, the Woman's Business, is frequently heard to say: "My boys are in college; they do not need me. My girls are married or at work, and they do not need me. I have nothing to do. My business is complete, I am retired, sidetracked. It is for this reason that I ask a part in politics." But her argument proves that she does not understand her business. She may want and need some outside occupation for the very health of her business, politics perhaps, but certainly not because her business is done.

There is no more critical time for her than when her young people go out to try themselves in the world. The girl particularly needs this pull of the home, not only to keep her on a straight path, but to keep her from the narrowness and selfishness which overtake so many self-supporting women who have no close family responsibilities. The fetich which has been made, for many years now, of work for women, that is, of work outside of the home, frequently leads the woman to take some particular virtue to herself for self-support. She feels that it entitles her to special consideration, releases her from obligations which she does not voluntarily assume. The attitude is enough to narrow and harden her life. The great preventive of this disaster is a responsible home relation. If she must share her earnings, it is a blessed thing for her. If not, she should share its burdens and its hopes, in order to have a continued source of outside interest to broaden and soften her, to keep her out of the ranks of the charmless, self-centered, single women, whose only occupations are self-support and self-care.

The problems involved in keeping the girl who has a home from being homeless are not simple. They are as intricate as anything a woman can face. They call for the highest understanding, responsiveness, and activity. No futile devices will meet them. "My daughter is not coming home to be idle," I heard a fine-intentioned woman say recently. "I insist that she take all the care of her room, save the weekly cleaning, and that she keep the living-room tidy." But what an occupation for a young woman with a college degree, who for four years has led a busy, well-organized life in which each task was directed toward some definite purpose! What a commentary on the mother's understanding of "economic independence," a matter of which she talks eloquently at her club! All that it proved was that the woman had never realized the girl's case, had never given consecutive, serious thought to its handling.

How little chance there will probably be for this same girl to do at home any serious work in case she develops a talent for it. The home of the prosperous, energetic American woman is pervaded by a spirit of eager and generally happy excitement. Good works and gay pleasures fill its days in a wild jumble. There is little or no order, selection, or discretion discernible in the result. "Something doing" all the time seems to be the motto, and to take part in this headless procession of unrelated events becomes the first law of the household. The daughter has been living an organized life in college. She wants to study or write, or do regular work of some kind. But there is no order in the spirit of the place, no respect for order, no respect for a regular occupation. "I cannot work at home"--one hears the cry often enough. It is not always because of this atmosphere of helter-skelter activity. It is often because of something worse,--an atmosphere of slothful, pleasure-loving indifference to activities of all kinds, or one of tacit or expressed discontent with the burdens and the limitations which are an inescapable part of the Business of Being a Woman.

The problems connected with a girl's desire to be of social service are even more difficult. There is a curious blindness or indifference in our town and country districts to social needs. There is still alive the notion that sending flowers and jellies to the hospital, distributing old clothes wisely, and packing generous Christmas baskets meet all obligations. Social service--of which one may, and generally does, hear a great deal in the women's clubs--is vaguely supposed to be something which has to do with great cities and factory towns, not with the small community. Yet one reason that social problems are so acute in great groups of men and women is that they are so poorly met in small and scattered groups. There is the same need of industrial training, of efficient schools, of books, of neighborliness, of innocent amusements, of finding opportunities for the exceptional child, of looking after the adenoids and teeth, of segregating the tubercular, of doing all the scores of social services in the small town as in the great. Work is really more hopeful there because there is some possibility of knowing approximately all the cases, which is never possible in the city. And yet how far from general it is to find anything like organized efforts at real social service in the small community. If a girl serves in such a community, it is because she has the parts of a pioneer--and few have.

It is not the girl who, having a home, yet is homeless, who is responsible for her situation. Her necessity is to see herself acting as a responsible and useful factor in an intelligent plan. If the family does not present itself to her as a grave, dignified undertaking on which several persons dear to her have embarked, how can she be expected to tie to it? The old phrases which she may hear now and then--"the honor of the family"--"duty to parents"--only savor of cant to her. They have no pricking vitality in them. She gets no acute reaction from them. She sees herself merely as an accident in an accidental group, headed nowhere in particular.

What it all amounts to is that the greatest art in the Woman's Business is using youth. It is no easy matter. Youth is a terrible force, confident, selfish, unknowing. Rarely has it real courage, real interest in aught but itself. It has all to learn, but it is youth, the most beautiful and hopeful thing in life. And it is the thing upon which the full development of life for a woman depends. She must have it always at her side, if she is to know her own full meaning in the scheme of things. It is part of her tragedy that she fails so often to understand how essential is youth to her as an individual, her happiness and her growth.

The fact that a woman is childless is no reason in the present world why she should be cut off from the developing and ennobling association. Indeed, the childless woman of to-day, in addition to her obligation to herself, has a peculiar obligation to society in the matter of the friendless child.

CHAPTER VIII

THE CHILDLESS WOMAN AND THE FRIENDLESS CHILD

One of the first conclusions forced on a thoughtful unprejudiced observer of society is that the major percentage of its pains and its vices result from a failure to make good connections. Children pine and even die for fruit in the cities, while a hundred miles away thousands of barrels of apples are rotting on the ground. Famine devastates one country, while the granaries of another are bursting with food. Men and women drink themselves into the gutter from sheer loneliness, while other men and women shrivel up in isolated comfort. One of the most pitiful examples of this failure to connect is that of the childless woman and the friendless, uncared-for child.

There never at any time in any country in the world's history existed so large a group of women with whom responsibility and effort were a matter of choice, as exists to-day in the United States. While a large number of these free women are devoting themselves whole-heartedly to public service of the most intelligent and ingenious kind, the great majority recognize no obligation to make any substantial return to society for its benefits. A small percentage of these are self-supporting, but the majority are purely parasitical. Indeed, the heaviest burden to-day on productive America, aside from the burden imposed by a vicious industrial system, is that of its nonproductive women. They are the most demanding portion of our society. They spend more money than any other group, are more insistent in their cry for amusement, are more resentful of interruptions of their pleasures and excitements; they go to greater extremes of indolence and of uneasiness.

The really serious side to the existence of this parasitical group is that great numbers of other women, not free, forced to produce, accept their standards of life. We hear women, useful women, everywhere talking about the desirability of not being obliged to do anything, commiserating women who must work, commiserating those who have heavy household responsibilities, and by the whole gist of their words and acts influencing those younger and less experienced than themselves to believe that happiness lies in irresponsible living.

Various gradations of the theory of which this is the extreme expression show themselves. Thus there are great numbers of women of moderate means, who by a little daily effort can keep comfortable and attractive homes for themselves and their husbands, and yet who are utterly regardless of outside responsibilities, who are practically isolated in the community. They pass their lives in a little round of household activities, sunning and preening themselves in their long hours of leisure like so many sleek cats.

There is still another division of this irresponsible class, who build up frenzied existences for themselves in all sorts of outside activities. They plunge headlong into each new proposition for pleasure or social service only to desert it as something more novel and exciting and, for the instant, popular, appears. Steady, intelligent standing by an undertaking through its ups and downs, its dull seasons and its unpopular phases, they are incapable of. Their efforts have no relation to an intelligently conceived purpose. With them may be grouped those women who, by their canonization of the unimportant, construct heavily burdened but utterly fruitless lives. They laboriously pad out their days with trivial things, vanities, shams, and shadows, to which they give the serious undivided attention which should be bestowed only on real enterprises.

There are others who seek soporifics, release from a hearty tackling of their individual situations, in absorbing work, a work which perhaps fills their minds, but which is mere occupation--something to make them forget--not an art for art's sake, not labor for its useful fruits, but a protective, separating shield to shut out the insistent demands of life in the place where they find themselves.

All of these women are rightfully classed as irresponsible, whether they are moved by vanity, indolence, purposelessness, social blindness, or, most pitiful, a sense of the emptiness of life unattended by the imagination which reveals the sources from which life is filled. No one of them is building a "House of Life" for herself. They are building gimcrack palaces, gingerbread cottages, structures which the first full blast of life will level to the ground.

These women are not peculiar to city or to country. They are scattered nation-wide. You find them on farms and in mansions, in offices and in academic halls. In startling contrast there exists almost under the very eaves of the roofs which shelter them a vast and pitiful group of friendless children,--the deserted babe, the "little mother," the boys and girls running wild on side streets in every village in our land and in every slum in the cities, the factory child, the shop girl who has no home. Let us remember that a goodly percentage of those at work have homes and that they are engaged in a stimulating, if hard, effort to "help," that they have the steadying consciousness that they are needed. Nevertheless, this mass of youth is on the whole in an unnatural position--an antisocial relation.

Society can never run rightfully until all its members are performing their natural functions. No woman, whatever her condition, can escape her obligation to youth without youth suffering, and without suffering herself. One of the crying needs of to-day is a crusade, a jar, which will force upon our free women the friendless children of the country, give them some sense of the undeniable relation they bear to them, show them that they are in a sense the cause of this pathetic group and that it is their work to relieve it.

True, for a woman there is nothing more painful than putting herself face to face with the suffering of children. Yet for many years now we have had in this country a large and increasing number who were going through the daily pain of grappling with every phase of the distressing problems which come from the poverty, friendlessness, and overwork of the young. Out of their heartbreaking scrutinies there have come certain determinations which are being adopted rapidly wherever the social sense is aroused. We may roughly sum up these conclusions or determinations to be these:--

It is not necessary or endurable that children grow up starved and overworked, that boys and girls be submitted to vicious surroundings, that talent be crushed, that young men and young women be devoured by crime and greed. Youth, its nurturing and developing, has become the passion of the day. This is the meaning of our bureaus of Child Labor, of our Children's Courts, our Houses of Correction, our Fresh-Air Funds and Vacation Homes, our laws regulating hours and conditions, our Social Settlements.

At its very best, however, legislation, organization, work in groups, only indirectly reach the base of the trouble. These homeless babes and children, these neglected boys and girls, these reckless shop and factory girls, are generally the pain and menace that they are because they have not had, as individuals, that guidance and affection of women to which each has a natural right. No collective work, however good it may be, can protect or guide these children properly. Rightfully they should be the charge of that body of women who are unhampered, "free." These women have more, or less, intelligence, time, and means. They owe society a return for their freedom, their means, and their education. Nature has made them the guardians of childhood. Can they decently shirk the obligation any more than a man can decently shirk his duty as a citizen? Indeed, the case of the woman unresponsive to her duty toward youth is parallel to that of the man unresponsive to his duty toward public affairs. One is as profitless and parasitical as the other.

The man who has no notion of what is doing politically in his own ward, who does not sense the malign influences which may be working in his neighborhood, in his very street, perhaps in the next house, who has not his eye on the unscrupulous small politician who leads the ward by the nose, who knows nothing of the records of the local candidates, never goes to the primaries,--this man is one of the most dangerous citizens we have. It is he who makes the machine possible. If he did his work, the governmental machine, which starts there with him, would be sound. It would be begun by honest men interested in serving the country to the best of their ability, and on such a foundation no future solidarity of corruption would be possible.

The individual woman's obligation toward the children and young people in her neighborhood is very like this obligation of the man to public affairs. It is for her to know the conditions under which the children, the boys and girls, young men and maids, in her vicinity are actually living. It is for her to be alert to their health, amusements, and general education. It is for her to find the one--and there always is one--that actually needs her. It is for her to correlate her personal discoveries and experiences with the general efforts of the community.

This is no work for an occasional morning. It does not mean sporadic or even regular "neighborhood visiting." It means observation, reflection, and study. It has nothing to do save indirectly with societies, or groups, or laws. It is a personal work, something nobody else can do, and something which, if it is neglected, adds just so much more to the stream of uncared-for youth. How is it to be done? Have you ever watched a woman interested in birds making her observations? She will get up at daylight to catch a note of a new singer. She will study in detail the little family that is making its home on her veranda. From the hour that the birds arrive in the spring until the hour that they leave in the fall she misses nothing of their doings. It is a beautiful and profitable study, and it is a type of what is required of a woman who would fulfill her obligation toward the youth of her neighborhood.

Could we have such study everywhere in country and town, what tragedies and shames we might be spared! A few months ago the whole nation was horrified by a riot in a prosperous small city of the Middle West which ended in the lynching of a young man, a mere boy, who in trying to discharge his duty as a public official had killed a man. Some thirty persons, over half of them boys under twenty years of age, are to-day serving terms of from fifteen to twenty years in the penitentiary for their part in this lynching.

Their terrible work was no insane outbreak. Analyzed, it was a logical consequence of the social and political conditions under which the boys had been brought up. In a pretty, rich, busy town of 30,000 people proud of its churches and its schools, eighty saloons industriously plied their business-- and part of their business, as it always is, was to train youths to become their patrons.

What were the women doing in the town? I asked the question of one who knew it. "Why," he said, "they were doing just what women do everywhere, no better, no worse. They had their clubs; I suppose a dozen literary clubs, several sewing clubs, several bridge clubs, and a number of dancing clubs. I think they cared a little more for bridge than for literature, many of them at least. They took little part in civic work, though they had done much for the city library and city hospital. Many girls went to college, to the State Institute, to Vassar and Smith. They came back to teach and to marry. It was just as it is everywhere."

Another to whom I put the same question, answered me in a sympathetic letter full of understanding comment. The mingled devotion, energy, and blindness of the women the letter described, spoke in its every line. They built charming homes, reared healthy, active children whom they educated at any personal sacrifice--all within a circle of eighty saloons! To offset the saloons they built churches--a church for each sect--each more gorgeous than its neighbor. It was in building churches that they showed the "greatest tenacity of purpose." They had a large temperance organization. It supported a rest room and met fortnightly to pray "ardently and sincerely." How little this body of good women sensed their problem, how little they were fitted to deal with it, my informant's comment reveals. "You doubtless remember the story," the letter runs, "of the old lady who deplored the shooting of craps because, though she didn't know what they were, 'life was probably as dear to them as to anybody.'"

"It was just as it is everywhere." Busy with self and their immediate circles, they went their daily ways unseeing, though these ways were hedged with a corruption whose rank and horrible offshoots at every step clutched the feet of the children for whom they were responsible.

Perhaps there is nothing to-day needed in this country more than driving into the minds of women this personal obligation to do what may be called intensive gardening in youth. Whether a woman wishes to see it or not, she is the center of a whirl of life. The health, the happiness, and the future of those that are in this whirl are affected vitally by what she is and does. To know all of the elements which are circulating about her as a man knows, if he does his work, the political and business elements in his own group, this is her essential task. That she should adjust her discoveries to the organizations, political, educational, and religious, which are about her, goes without saying, but these organizations are not the heart of her matter. The heart of her matter lies in what she does for those who come into immediate contact with her.

Her business firmly established in her immediate group should grow as a man's business does in the outer circle where he naturally operates. It will become stable or unstable exactly as trade or profession becomes stable or unstable. Every year it should take on new elements, ramify, turn up new obligations, knit itself more firmly into the life of the community. With every year it should become necessarily more complicated, broader in interests, more demanding on her intellectual and spiritual qualities. Each one of the original members of her group gathers others about himself. In the nature of the case she will become one of the strongest influences in these new groups. As a member goes out she will project herself into other communities or perhaps other lands, into all sorts of industries, professions, and arts. Her growth is absolutely natural. It is, too, one of the most economical growths the world knows. Nothing is lost in it. She spreads literally like the banyan tree.

Yet in spite of this perfectly obvious fact, there are people to-day asking, with all appearance of sincerity, what a woman of fifty or more can do! Their confining work in the home, say these observers, is done. A common suggestion is that they be utilized in politics. This suggestion has its comical side. A person who has nothing to do after fifty years of life in a business as many-sided and demanding as that of a woman, can hardly be expected to be worth much in a business as complicated and uncertain as politics, and for which she has had no training. The notion that the woman's business is ended at fifty or sixty is fantastic. It only ends there if she has been blind to the meaning of her own experiences; if she has never gone below the surface of her task--never seen in it anything but physical relations and duties; has sensed none of its intimate relations to the community, none of its obligations toward those who have left her, none of those toward the oncoming generations. If it ends there, she has failed to realize, too, the tremendous importance to all those who belong in her circle or who touch it of what she makes of herself, of her personal achievement.

A woman of fifty or sixty who has succeeded, has come to a point of sound philosophy and serenity which is of the utmost value in the mental and spiritual development of the group to which she belongs. Life at every one of its seven stages has its peculiar harrowing experiences; hope mingles with uncertainty in youth; fear and struggle characterize early manhood; disillusionment, the question whether it is worth while, fill the years from forty to fifty,--but resolute grappling with each period brings one out almost inevitably into a fine serene certainty which cannot but have its effect on those who are younger. Ripe old age, cheerful, useful, and understanding, is one of the finest influences in the world. We hang Rembrandt's or Whistler's picture of his mother on our walls that we may feel its quieting hand, the sense of peace and achievement which the picture carries. We have no better illustration of the meaning of old age.

Family and social groups should be a blend of all ages. One of the present weaknesses of our society is that we herd each age together. The young do not have enough of the stimulating intellectual influence of their elders. The elders do not have enough of the vitalizing influence of the young. We make up our dinner party according to age, with the result that we lose the full, fine blend of life.

The notion that a woman has no worthy place or occupation after she is fifty or sixty, and that she can be utilized in public affairs, could only be entertained by one who has no clear conception of either private or public affairs--no vision of the infinite reaches of the one or the infinite complexities of the other. Human society may be likened to two great circles, one revolving within the other. In the inner circle rules the woman. Here she breeds and trains the material for the outer circle, which exists only by and for her. That accident may throw her into this outer circle is of course true, but it is not her natural habitat, nor is she fitted by nature to live and circulate freely there. We underestimate, too, the kind of experience which is essential for intelligent citizenship in this outer circle. To know what is wise and needed there one should circulate in it. The man at his labor in the street, in the meeting places of men, learns unconsciously, as a rule, the code, the meaning, the need of public affairs as woman learns those of private affairs. What it all amounts to is that the labor of the world is naturally divided between the two different beings that people the world. It is unfair to the woman that she be asked to do the work of the outer circle. The man can do that satisfactorily if she does her part; that is, if she prepares him the material. Certainly, he can never come into the inner circle and do her work.

The idea that there is a kind of inequality for a woman in minding her own business and letting man do the same, comes from our confused and rather stupid notion of the meaning of equality. Popularly we have come to regard being alike as being equal. We prove equality by wearing the same kind of clothes, studying the same books, regardless of nature or capacity or future life. Insisting that women do the same things that men do, may make the two exteriorly more alike--it does not make them more equal. Men and women are widely apart in functions and in possibilities. They cannot be made equal by exterior devices like trousers, ballots, the study of Greek. The effort to make them so is much more likely to make them unequal. One only comes to his highest power by following unconsciously and joyfully his own nature. We run the risk of destroying the capacity for equality when we attempt to make one human being like another human being.

The theory that the class of free women considered here would be fired to unselfish interest in uncared-for youth if they were included in the electorate of the nation is hardly sustainable. The ballot has not prevented the growth of a similar class of men. Something more biting than a new tool is needed to arouse men and women who are absorbed in self--some poignant experience which thrusts upon their indolent minds and into their restricted visions the actualities of life.

It should be said, however, that the recent agitation for the ballot has served as such an experience for a good many women, particularly in the East. Perhaps for the first time they have heard from the suffrage platform of the "little mother," the factory child, the girl living on $6 a week. They have done more than espouse the suffrage cause for the sake of the child; they have gone out to find where they could serve.

It is a new knowledge of that tide of life which breaks at her very gate that the childless and the free American woman needs, if she is to discharge her obligation to the uncared-for child. To force these facts upon her, to cry to her, "You are the woman,--you cannot escape the guilt of the woe and crime which must come from the neglect of childhood in your radius,"--this is the business of every man and woman who has had the pain and the privilege of seeing something of the actual life of the people of this world.

CHAPTER IX

ON THE ENNOBLING OF THE WOMAN'S BUSINESS

That the varied, delicate, and difficult problems which crowd the attention of the woman in her social laboratory should ever be considered unworthy of first-class brains and training is but proof of the difficulty the human mind has in distinguishing values when in the throes of social change. We rightly believe to-day that the world is not nearly so well run as it would be if we could--or would--apply unselfishly what we already know. Each of us advocates his own pet theory of betterment, often to the exclusion of everybody else's theory.

One of the most disconcerting characteristics of advocates, conservative and radical, is their conscienceless treatment of facts. Rarely do they allow full value to that which qualifies or contradicts their theories. The ardent and single-minded reformer is not infrequently the worst sinner in this respect. To stir indignation against conditions, he paints them without a background and with utter disregard of proportion.

He wins, but he loses, by this method. He makes converts of those of his own kind, those who like him have rare powers for indignation and sacrifice, but little capacity or liking for the exact truth or for self-restraint. He turns from him many who are as zealous as he to change conditions, but who demand that they be painted as they are and that justice be rendered both to those who have fought against them in the past and to those who are in different ways doing so to-day.

The movement for a fuller life for American women has always suffered from the disregard of some of its noblest followers, both for things as they are and for things as they have been. The persistent belittling for campaign purposes of the Business of Being a Woman I have repeatedly referred to in this little series of essays; indeed, it has been founded on the proposition that the Uneasy Woman of to-day is to a large degree the result of the belittlement of her natural task and that her chief need is to dignify, make scientific, professionalize, that task.

I doubt if there is to-day a more disintegrating influence at work--one more fatal to sound social development--than that which belittles the home and the position of the woman in it. As a social institution nothing so far devised by man approaches the home in its opportunity, nor equals it in its successes.

The woman's position at its head is hard. The result of her pains and struggles are rarely what she hopes, either for herself or for any one connected with her, but this is true of all human achievement. There is nothing done that does not mean self-denial, routine, disillusionment, and half realization. Even the superman goes the same road, coming out at the same halfway-up house! It is the meaning of the effort, not the half result, that counts.

The pain and struggle of an enterprise are not what takes the heart out of a soldier; it is telling him his cause is mean, his fight in vain. Show him a reason, and he dies exultant. The woman is the world's one permanent soldier. After all war ceases she must go daily to her fight with death. To tell her this giving of her life for life is merely a "female function," not a human part, is to talk nonsense and sacrilege. It is the clear conviction of even the most thoughtless girl that this way lies meaning and fulfillment of life, that gives her courage to go to her battle as a man-in-line to his, and like him she comes out with a new understanding. The endless details of her life, its routine and its restraints, have a reason now, as routine and discipline have for a soldier. She sees as he does that they are the only means of securing the victory bought so dearly--of winning others.

From this high conviction the great mass of women never have and never can be turned. What does happen constantly, however, is loss of joy and courage in their undertaking. When these go, the vision goes. The woman feels only her burdens, not the big meaning in them. She remembers her daily grind, not the possibilities of her position. She falls an easy victim now to that underestimation of her business which is so popular. If she is of gentle nature, she becomes apologetic, she has "never done anything." If she is aggressive, she becomes a militant. In either case, she charges her dissatisfaction to the nature of her business. What has come to her is a common human experience, the discovery that nothing is quite what you expected it to be, that if hope is to be even halfway realized, it will be by courage and persistency. It is not the woman's business that is at fault; it is the faulty handling of it and the human difficulty in keeping heart when things grow hard. What she needs is a strengthening of her wavering faith in her natural place in the world, to see her business as a profession, its problems formulated and its relations to the work of society, as a whole, clearly stated.

Quite as great an injustice to her as the belittling of her business has been the practice, also for campaigning purposes, of denying her a part in the upbuilding of civilization. There was a time "back of history," says one of the popular leaders in the Woman's movement, "when men and women were friends and comrades--but from that time to this she (woman) has held a subsidiary and exclusively feminine position. The world has been wholly in the hands of men, and they have believed that men alone had the ability, felt the necessity, for developing civilization, the business, education, and religion of the world."

Women's present aim she declares to be the "reassumption of their share in human life." This is, of course, a modern putting of the List of Grievances with which the militant campaign started in this country in the 40's, re 雜 forced by the important point that women "back of history" enjoyed the privileges which the earlier militants declared that man, "having in direct object the establishment of an absolute tyranny over her," had always usurped.

Just how the lady knows that "back of history" women and men were more perfect comrades than to-day, I do not know. Her proofs would be interesting. If this is true, it reverses the laws which have governed all other human relations. Certainly, since history began, the only period where I can pretend to judge what has happened, the records show that comradeship between men and women has risen and fallen with the rise and fall of cultivation and of virtue. The general level is probably higher to-day than ever before.

Moreover, from these same records one might support as plausibly--and as falsely--the theory of a Woman-made World as the popular one of a Man-made World. There has been many a teacher and philosopher who has sustained some form of this former thesis, disclaiming against the excessive power of women in shaping human affairs. The teachings of the Christian Church in regard to women, the charge that she keep silent, that she obey, that she be meek and lowly--all grew out of the fear of the power she exercised at the period these teachings were given--a power which the saints believed prejudicial to good order and good morals. There is more than one profound thinker of our own period who has arraigned her influence--Strindberg and Nietzsche among them. You cannot turn a page of history that the woman is not on it or behind it. She is the most subtle and binding thread in the pattern of Human Life!

For the American Woman of to-day to allow woman's part in the making of this nation to be belittled is particularly unjust and cowardly. The American nation in its good and evil is what it is, as much because of its women as because of its men. The truth of the matter is, there has never been any country, at any time, whatever may have been their social limitations or political disbarments, that women have not ranked with the men in actual capacity and achievement; that is, men and women have risen and fallen together, whatever the apparent conditions. The failure to recognize this is due either to ignorance of facts or to a willful disregard of them; usually it is the former. For instance, one constantly hears to-day the exultant cry that women finally are beginning to take an interest and a part in political and radical discussions. But there has never been a time in this country's history when they were not active factors in such discussion. The women of the American Revolutionary Period certainly challenge sharply the women of to-day, both by their intelligent understanding of political issues and by their sympathetic co 鰭 eration in the struggle. It was the letters of women which led to that most important factor in centralizing and instructing pre-revolutionary opinion in New England, the Committee of Correspondence. There were few more powerful political pamphleteers in that period than Mercy Warren. We might very well learn a lesson which we need very much to learn from the way women aided the Revolutionary cause through their power as consumers. As for sacrifice and devotion, that of the woman loses nothing in nobility when contrasted with that of the man.

If we jump fifty years in the nation's history to the beginning of the agitation against slavery, we find women among the first and most daring of the protestants against the institution. It was for the sake of shattering slavery that they broke the silence in public which by order of the Christian Church they had so long kept--an order made, not for the sake of belittling women, but for the sake of establishing order in churches and better insuring the new Christian code of morality. The courage and the radicalism of women of the 30's, 40's, and 50's in this country compare favorably with that of the men and women in any revolutionary period in any country that we may select.

The American woman has played an honorable part in the making of our country, and for this part she should have full credit. If she had been as poor a stick, as downtrodden and ineffective as sometimes painted, she would not be a fit mate for the man beside whom she has struggled, and she would be as utterly unfit for the larger life she desires as the most bigoted misogynist pictures her to be.

Moreover, all things considered, she has been no greater sufferer from injustice than man. I do not mean in saying this that she has not had grave and unjust handicaps, legal and social; I mean that when you come to study the comparative situations of men and women as a mass at any time and in any country you will find them more nearly equal than unequal, all things considered. Women have suffered injustice, but parallel have been the injustices men were enduring. It was not the fact that she was a woman that put her at a disadvantage so much as the fact that might made right, and the physically weaker everywhere bore the burden of the day. Go back no further than the beginnings of this Republic and admit all that can be said of the wrong in the laws which prevented a woman controlling the property she had inherited or accumulated by her own efforts, which took from her a proper share in the control of her child,--we must admit, too, the equal enormity of the laws which permitted man to exploit labor in the outrageous way he has. It was not because he was a man that the labor was exploited--it was because he was the weaker in the prevailing system. Woman's case was parallel--she was the weaker in the system. It had always been the case with men and women in the world that he who could took and the devil got the hindermost. The way the laborer's cause has gone hand in hand in this country the last hundred years with the woman's cause is a proof of the point. In the 30's of the nineteenth century, for illustration, the country was torn by a workingman's party which carried on a fierce agitation against banks and monopolies. Many of its leaders were equally ardent in their support of Women's Rights as they were then understood. The slavery agitation was coupled from the start with the question of Women's Rights. It was injustice that was being challenged--the right of the stronger to put the weaker at a disadvantage for any reason--because he was poor, not rich; black, not white; female, not male,--that is, there has been nothing special to women in the injustice she has suffered except its particular form. Moreover, it was not man alone who was responsible for this injustice. Stronger women have often imposed upon the weak--men and women--as strong men have done. In its essence, it is a human, not a sex, question--this of injustice.

The hesitation of this country in the earlier part of the nineteenth century to accord to women the same educational facilities as to men is often cited as a proof of a deliberate effort to disparage women. But it should not be forgotten that the wisdom of universal male education was hotly in debate. One of the ideals of radical reformers for centuries had been to give to all the illumination of knowledge. But to teach those who did the labor of the world, its peasants and its serfs, was regarded by both Church and State as a folly and a menace. It was the establishment of a pure democracy that forced the experiment of universal free instruction in this country. It has met with opposition at every stage, and there is to-day a Mr. Worldly Wiseman at every corner bewailing the evils it has wrought. He must, too, be a hopeless Candide who can look on our experiment, wonderful and inspiring as it is, and say its results have been the best possible.

It was entirely logical, things beings as they were, that there should have been strong opposition to giving girls the same training in schools as boys. That objection holds good to-day in many reflective minds. He again must be a hopeless optimist who believes that we have worked out the best possible system of education for women. But that there was opposition to giving women the same educational facilities as men was not saying that there was or ever had been a conspiracy on foot to keep her in intellectual limbo because she was a woman. The history of learning shows clearly enough that women have always shared in its rise. In the great revival of the sixteenth century they took an honorable part. "I see the robbers, hangmen, adventurers, hostlers of to-day more learned than the doctors and preacher of my youth," wrote Rabelais, and he added, "why, women and girls have aspired to the heavenly manna of good learning." Whenever aspiration has been in the air, women have responded to it as men have, and have found, as men have found, a way to satisfy their thirst.

To come down to the period which concerns us chiefly, that of our own Republic, it is an utter misrepresentation of the women of the Revolution to claim that they were uneducated. All things considered, they were quite as well educated as the men. The actual achievements of the eminent women produced by the system of training then in vogue is proof enough of the statement. Far and away the best letters by a woman, which have found their way into print in this country, are those of Mrs. John Adams, written late in the eighteenth century and early in the nineteenth. They deserve the permanent place in our literature which they have. But it was a period of good letter writing by women--if weak spelling and feminine spelling was, on the whole, quite as strong as masculine!

Out of that early system of education came the woman who was to write the book which did more to stir the country against slavery than all that ever had been written, Harriet Beecher Stowe. That system produced the scientist, who still represents American women in the mind of the world, Maria Mitchell, the only American woman whose name appears among the names of the world's great scholars inscribed on the Boston Public Library. It produced Dorothea Dix, who for twenty years before the Civil War carried on perhaps the most remarkable investigation of conditions that has ever been made in this country by man or woman,--the one which required the most courage, endurance, and persistency,--her investigation of the then barbaric system for caring--or not caring--for the insane. State after state enacted new laws and instituted new methods solely on the showing of this one woman. If there were no other case to offer to the frequent cry that women have never had an influence on legislation, this would be enough. Moreover, this is but the most brilliant example of the kind of work women had been doing from the beginning of the Republic.

To my mind there is no phase of their activities which reveals better the genuineness of their training than the initiative they took in founding schools of advanced grades for girls, and in organizing primary and secondary schools on something like a national scale. Mary Lyon's work for Mt. Holyoke College and Catherine Beecher's for the American Woman's Education Association are the most substantial individual achievements, though they are but types of what many women were doing and what women in general were backing up. It was work of the highest constructive type--original in its conception, full of imagination and idealism, rich in its capacity for growth--a work to fit the aspiration of its day and so full of the future!

Now, when conditions are such that a few rise to great eminence from the ordinary ranks of life, it means a good general average. The multitude of women of rare achievements, distinguishing the Revolutionary and post-Revolutionary periods of American history are the best evidences of the seriousness, idealism, and intelligence of the women in general. Their services in the war are part of the traditions of every family whose line runs back to those days. Loyal, spirited, ingenious, and uncomplaining, they are one of the finest proofs in history of the capacity of the women of the mass to respond whole-heartedly to noble ideals,--one of the finest illustrations, too, of the type of service needed from women in great crises. But the rank and file which conducted itself so honorably in the Revolution was not a whit more noble and intelligent than the rank and file of the succeeding period. It would have been impossible ever to have established as promptly as was done the higher and the general schools for girls if women had not given them the support they did, had not been willing, as one great educator of the early part of the nineteenth century has recorded--"to rise up early, to sit up late, to eat the bread of the most rigid economy, that their daughters might be favored with means of improvement superior to what they themselves possessed." And back of this self-denial was what? A desire that life be made easier for the daughter? Not at all--a desire that the daughter be better equipped to "form the character of the future citizen of the Republic."

It is not alone that justice is wounded by denying women a part in the making of the civilized world--a more immediate wrong is the way the movement for a fuller, freer life for all human beings is hampered. A woman with a masculine chip on her shoulder gives a divided attention to the cause she serves. She complicates her human fight with a sex fight. However good tactics this may have been in the past, and I am far from denying that there were periods it may have been good politics, however poor morals, surely in this country to-day there is no sound reason for introducing such complications into our struggles. The American woman's life is the fullest in its opportunity, all things considered, that any human beings harnessed into a complicated society have ever enjoyed. To keep up the fight against man as the chief hindrance to the realization of her aspiration is merely to perpetuate in the intellectual world that instinct of the female animal to be ever on guard against the male, save in those periods when she is in pursuit of him!

But complicating her problem is not the only injury she does her cause by this ignoring or belittling of woman's part in civilization. She strips herself of suggestion and inspiration--a loss that cannot be reckoned. The past is a wise teacher. There is none that can stir the heart more deeply or give to human affairs such dignity and significance. The meaning of woman's natural business in the world--the part it has played in civilizing humanity--in forcing good morals and good manners, in giving a reason and so a desire for peaceful arts and industries, the place it has had in persuading men and women that only self-restraint, courage, good cheer, and reverence produce the highest types of manhood and womanhood,--this is written on every page of history.

Women need the ennobling influence of the past. They need to understand their integral part in human progress. To slur this over, ignore, or deny it, cripples their powers. It sets them at the foolish effort of enlarging their lives by doing the things man does--not because they are certain that as human beings with a definite task they need--or society needs--these particular services or operations from them, but because they conceive that this alone will prove them equal. The efforts of woman to prove herself equal to man is a work of supererogation. There is nothing he has ever done that she has not proved herself able to do equally well. But rarely is society well served by her undertaking his activities. Moreover, if man is to remain a civilized being, he must be held to his business of producer and protector. She cannot overlook her obligation to keep him up to his part in the partnership, and she cannot wisely interfere too much with that part. The fate of the meddler is common knowledge!

A few women in every country have always and probably always will find work and usefulness and happiness in exceptional tasks. They are sometimes women who are born with what we call "bachelor's souls"--an interesting and sometimes even charming, though always an incomplete, possession! More often they are women who by the bungling machinery of society have been cast aside. There is no reason why these women should be idle, miserable, selfish, or antisocial. There are rich lives for them to work out and endless needs for them to meet. But they are not the women upon whom society depends; they are not the ones who build the nation. The women who count are those who outnumber them a hundred to one--the women who are at the great business of founding and filling those natural social centers which we call homes. Humanity will rise or fall as that center is strong or weak. It is the human core.

###